ST DIES IN R ...ORY

This series, specially commissioned by the Economic History Society, provides a guide to the current interpretations of the key themes of economic and social history in which advances have recently been made or in which there has been significant debate.

Originally entitled 'Studies in Economic History', in 1974 the series had its scope extended to include topics in social history, and the new series title, 'Studies in Economic and Social History', signalises this development.

The series gives readers access to the best work done, helps them to draw their own conclusions in major fields of study, and by means of the critical bibliography in each book guides them in the selection of further reading. The aim is to provide a springboard to further work rather than a set of pre-packaged conclusions or short-cuts.

ECONOMIC HISTORY SOCIETY

The Economic History Society, which numbers over 3000 members, publishes the *Economic History Review* four times a year (free to members) and holds an annual conference. Enquiries about membership should be addressed to the Assistant Secretary, Economic History Society, Peterhouse, Cambridge. Full-time students may join at special rates.

STUDIES IN ECONOMIC AND SOCIAL HISTORY

Edited for the Economic History Society by T. C. Smout

PUBLISHED

OTHER TITLES ARE IN PREPARATION

The English Woollen Industry
1500 – 1750

Prepared for
The Economic History Society by

G. D. RAMSAY

Emeritus Fellow
of St Edmund Hall, Oxford

© The Economic History Society 1982

All rights reserved. No part of this publication
may be reproduced or transmitted, in any form
or by any means, without permission.

First published 1982 by
THE MACMILLAN PRESS LTD
London and Basingstoke
Companies and representatives
throughout the world

Filmset in 10/12pt Compugraphic Baskerville by
Reproduction Drawings Ltd., Sutton, Surrey
Printed in Hong Kong

ISBN 0 333 191900

Contents

Preface

THIS small booklet contains a summary survey of a very large subject. Like other contributions to the series in which it appears, it makes no claim to be a work of first-hand research: it is frankly based on the labours of other historians and only occasionally on my own. To keep it short, much illustrative detail has been omitted, and the byways of industrial history avoided. While it is no part of my brief to write a general social or economic history, it may be hoped that readers will not find any corners cut.

My thanks are due to Professor M. W. Flinn and Professor T. C. Smout, successive editors of the series in which this little study appears, for their kindness and forbearance; and also to the anonymous reader who critically perused my typescript for the Economic History Society. I have given heed to his remarks. But errors and other shortcomings are all my own.

Oxford

G. D. RAMSAY

Editor's Preface

SINCE 1968, when the Economic History Society and Macmillan published the first of the 'Studies in Economic and Social History', the series has established itself as a major teaching tool in universities, colleges and schools, and as a familiar landmark in serious bookshops throughout the country. A great deal of the credit for this must go to the wise leadership of its first editor, Professor M. W. Flinn, who retired at the end of 1977. The books tend to be bigger now than they were originally, and inevitably more expensive; but they have continued to provide information in modest compass at a reasonable price by the standards of modern academic publications.

There is no intention of departing from the principles of the first decade. Each book aims to survey findings and discussion in an important field of economic or social history that has been the subject of recent lively debate. It is meant as an introduction for readers who are not themselves professional researchers but who want to know what the discussion is all about – students, teachers and others generally interested in the subject. The authors, rather than either taking a strongly partisan line or suppressing their own critical faculties, set out the arguments and the problems as fairly as they can, and attempt a critical summary and explanation of them from their own judgement. The discipline now embraces so wide a field in the study of the human past that it would be inappropriate for each book to follow an identical plan, but all volumes will normally contain an extensive descriptive bibliography.

The series is not meant to provide all the answers but to help readers to see the problems clearly enough to form their own conclusions. We shall never agree in history, but the discipline will be well served if we know what we are disagreeing about, and why.

T. C. SMOUT

Editor

University of St Andrews

I Manufacture

1 Processes and products

NEXT to food and shelter, in all parts of the world outside the tropics clothing is a requirement for human life. For almost all the year, north-west Europe would certainly be uninhabitable without it. Hence for uncountable centuries even before the Roman occupation of Gaul and Britain, sheep's wool was there being spun into yarn for weaving into cloth for garments. Long before AD 1500 this ancient industry had reached a high point of development in England, where it was practised over most of the country. A parliamentary statute of 1337[1] had encouraged and protected domestic clothmaking by forbidding the import of foreign woollen textiles. The only sources of competition were therefore those provided by furs and skins, too scarce for widespread use; linen, which was too light; and silk, which was too costly. Cotton was conveniently available as an alternative material for the clothmaker only from the very late sixteenth century; and its use for the production of textiles grew at the expense of the linen rather than the woollen industry. Thus during the quarter of a millennium covered by this survey, English manufactures had little rivalry to encounter in the home market.

The processes in the course of which the often dirty-looking fleece on the body of the sheep was transformed into a smooth, chill-proof garment for human beings to wear, involved the skills of more than a score of various craftsmen and half-a-dozen or more changes of ownership. The sheep themselves were in the care of the shepherd, sometimes a peasant with

9

some degree of independence, sometimes the servant of the landowner on whose estate they were pastured. The wool when shorn frequently passed through the hands of a wool-brogger (broker) who saw to its packing and mixing before selling it to the clothier who organised the manufacture into cloth. It was cleaned, oiled, sorted and carded (if short) or combed (if long) before it reached the spinner. In the form of yarn it was fed into the loom by the weaver, who achieved the crucial transformation into a piece of cloth ready for a further range of treatments. The newly woven fabric, scoured by fuller's earth, was thickened by the fuller or tucker, who steeped and battered it in a vat of urine. It was then affixed to a 'tenter' to dry. If in the course of these processes it had shrunk unduly, it might now be stretched to recover its proper dimensions. The nap was then raised by passing teasles, mounted on a frame, across the fabric, a process known as 'rowing' or 'barbing', after which a smooth surface was created by the shearmen who with a large and heavy pair of shears clipped off the fluff or rough wool. To improve the surface, the nap raising and shearing were several times repeated. If the wool had not already been given the desired colour before reaching the spinner it might be now that the cloth was plunged into the dyer's vat unless, like so much broadcloth in the sixteenth century, it was to be exported undyed and undressed.[2]

For the efficient application of these processes both skill and experience were desirable, but the formal apprenticeship to impart them was not uniformly enforced. Besides, techniques were constantly altering, though the pace of change was uneven. The horizontal loom, in general use throughout our period in England, had originated in China for use in the silk manufacture. It was introduced into Europe only in the eleventh century, after which it supplanted the ancient vertical loom in the woollen industry. The spinning wheel arrived likewise from the orient only a little later, and was used at first in Italy with cotton yarn.[3] The improved or 'Saxony' wheel for spinning was probably not known in England before the very late sixteenth century. The fulling mill, known in France in the eleventh century, came into widespread use in England during the thirteenth. Sporadic appearances of dubious devices indicated the persistence of the quest for technical improvement in cloth manufacture. The use of winches for stretching cloths was forbidden by law in 1552, because of the opportunities for deceit to which it gave rise.[4] There was a whole series of enactments to suppress or at least control the use of the 'tenters' on which cloths were fastened to dry after being fulled. Since the cloths tended naturally to shrink, a measure of 'tentering' was unavoidable; but there was a limit to the amount of stretching or pulling to which any piece might in fairness be subjected. A statute of 1483 allowed the hanging of cloths upon tenters to dry, though only in an open place where by implication the process might be observed;[5] but a sequence of repetitive enactments bore subsequent witness to the impossibility of eradicating excessive stretching in manufacture. Other legislation was directed against the gig-mill, sometimes known as the mozing-mill, when iron wire or nails replaced teasles for raising the nap. It was alleged to tear the fabric. Therefore, when in 1609 – 12 the sweated shearmen of Shrewsbury fought for the introduction of such a device to ease their labour, their paymasters, the drapers of the town, opposed them.

Probably more often, any new labour-saving gadgets met with hostility because of their threat to employment. No doubt there was much tinkering. The English by mid-eighteenth century had earned a reputation for 'their machines to abridge labour'; in this, silk and cotton tended as in the middle ages to precede wool. As early as 1678, a patent was taken out for a device to improve the productivity of spinners, but like other inventions it proved still-born. The 'Dutch loom' for ribbon-making, the silk throwster's mill in service in early eighteenth-century Derbyshire and the flying shuttle invented by Kay in 1730 were notable because they survived.[6] But the most striking early invention was the stocking-frame contrived by the clergyman William Lee in the late sixteenth century. It persisted in use and ultimately provided an essential stimulus for a specialised branch of the woollen industry. Hand-knitted stockings were a by-product of peasant households in the off-season, and were made in many counties. They became objects of commerce increasingly during the sixteenth century, winning a market at home and abroad. Lee presumably invented his stocking-frame so as to enable his Nottinghamshire parishioners to increase their output and so their income, though in the event his invention was first exploited to make silk stockings in London. Very gradually, the knitting-frame won acceptance in the north-east midlands, where the production of fine worsted stockings was stimulated in the seventeenth century mainly in Leicestershire, though also to a smaller extent in Nottinghamshire. Popular hostility helps to explain the slow and sometimes furtive way in which the knitting-frame crept into use, though it must be recalled that it was an elaborate and expensive machine comprising over two thousand pieces. For its profitable use both capital and skill were necessary, so that it is scarcely surprising that even as late as 1750 most stockings were still being knitted by hand –though this situation was soon to alter.

Most cloths in the sixteenth century were dyed only if destined for consumption at home, or in certain peripheral and relatively small foreign markets. To sell cloths abroad, it was the conventional wisdom that dyeing had better be deferred until they had been taken as far as the international market at Antwerp, where there were large numbers of craftsmen with special skills in dyeing and finishing, where the foreign merchant who bought the cloths might select the colour to suit his customers. Only from the early seventeenth century onwards were consumers on the nearby continent gradually to put aside their prejudices and wear cloths dyed in England. The dyestuffs traditionally in use from the earliest times were woad, madder and saffron, available either at home or from countries nearby; but from the late sixteenth century the much more powerful and brilliant tropical dyes, especially cochineal and indigo, were coming on the market. Cochineal was a monopoly product of Mexico, so that regular supplies were only assured with the Anglo-Spanish pacification of 1604. The best indigo came from certain districts of western India, but by the second quarter of the seventeenth century indigo was also being grown on the islands of the Caribbean. For fixing colours, the essential mordant was always alum, which was extracted from the mineral alunite. In the sixteenth century this was available from mines in Spain or, more importantly, from the great mine at Tolfa in papal territory near Rome. The Apostolic Chamber continued to draw revenue from sales of alum to the English, whatever their ecclesiastical allegiance, until the entrepreneur Sir Arthur Ingram succeeded in organising the profitable extraction of alum from mines in Yorkshire early in the seventeenth century.

A good deal is known about the sizes and weights of the woollen cloths commonly in production at mid-sixteenth century, thanks to the precise measurements specified in an elaborate statute of 1552.[7] Although the advent of the 'new draperies' lay in the future, nearly forty different sorts of cloth were already to be distinguished. They were mostly known after their original county of manufacture, though sometimes after a town or even a village: thus there were the types called 'Tauntons' and 'Bridgwaters', or 'Worcesters' short and long, or 'Manchester' rugs and friezes. But they fell into two main divisions. There were the broadcloths, which were large fabrics: the heaviest, which were made in Kent or Sussex or at Reading, were 28 to 30 yards in length and required to weigh at least 90 lb. Somewhat smaller varieties were produced in great quantity in the west country, the minimum weight for these being only 68 lb. It was reckoned at the time that each broadcloth embodied the clip of 45 to 60 sheep. The other division was the kersey, named after the Suffolk village of Kersey; but kerseys were made all over the country from Devonshire to the West Riding, with varying weights in each locality and sometimes with changes of nomenclature.[8] Kerseys were much smaller and lighter fabrics; three of them were usually equated at the customs to a broadcloth, or 'short cloth', as it was officially called. Both broadcloths and kerseys were frequently sold to the merchant in packs of ten, and obviously posed some problems of transport. Reading and Kentish broadcloths at least could travel to London by water.

The industry was anything but monotonous in the character of its output. Indeed, the products of English looms were constantly varying, though there was seldom anyone to monitor the changes. By the later sixteenth century, the geographical description of any cloth indicated not so much its

13

actual place of manufacture as its qualities: thus in the early 1590s the clothiers of Dorset were reported to have switched from the making of Devonshire 'dozens' to 'the Hampshire kerseys called Readings, or sorting kerseys'.[9] By this time, to take a further example 'Castle Combes' was rather a generic name, like 'Cotswold wool': it meant fine cloths like those made at Castle Combe in Wiltshire. The foreign customer would have known what this implied. Although the best English wool was becoming scarcer, quality cloths were finer and finer. From the early seventeenth century, the increasing import of fine Spanish wool encouraged the growth of a specialised branch of the industry whose products were somewhat confusingly known as 'Spanish cloths' because of the raw material from which they were woven, or woven in part. In the manufacturing process there were technical alterations prompted by the varieties of yarn to which looms had to be adjusted. The cotton, linen and silk industries lie outside the scope of this survey, and it is likely that their full impact as technical pace-setters upon the woollen manufacture was deferred until the advent of full mechanisation from the late eighteenth century onwards. But long before this happened, cloths were occasionally being made of mixed yarns, warp and weft being of different materials.

The starting point of sweeping changes in the English woollen industry is generally identified as the establishment, from the 1560s onwards, of the 'new drapery' manufacture. The 'new draperies' were relatively cheap cloths, lighter in texture than the traditional 'old draperies' and manufactured in pieces smaller even than kerseys. Lighter cloths, it is evident, were coming into fashion perhaps because more layers of clothing were being worn, or conceivably even because the diffusion of window glass in the late sixteenth and early seventeenth centuries was simplifying the problem of heating rooms and banishing draughts. But the new draperies were a response to problems of supply as well as of demand, for alterations in the quality of native English wool were also an element in precipitating change. The gradual transformation of the textile industry brought about by the new draperies was in part due to the chronic scarcity of fine English wool. This in

14

turn sprang from the sheep-breeders' preference for large animals with coarser fleeces which could better meet the needs of the urban butchers, above all of those in London. New draperies were not made of expensive March or Cotswold wool. They were fabrics of the worsted type, manufactured from the long-stapled wool now more readily available, and combed not carded before conversion into yarn. We may be certain that the new draperies did not flourish because the processes of their manufacture were labour saving or in some way more advanced, since the yarn they used was sometimes spun on the distaff and not on the spinning-wheel, and the fabrics when woven were sometimes fulled by trampling with human feet and not pounded at a water-mill. New draperies comprised many different varieties of cloths, of which serges have perhaps enjoyed the most persistent demand.

Caution is needed not to overstress the novelty of the new draperies. Worsted cloths had long been made in Norfolk and elsewhere. Besides, a continuous and reciprocal interaction always linked English and continental styles of clothmaking: to balance the advent of the new draperies there were the occasional alarms at news that English artificers were being lured abroad to establish the manufacture of broadcloths and kerseys in the Netherlands or Italy. However, there is no denying that the arrival of immigrants from the Netherlands c. 1560 opened wider the gates of change in the textile industry. The newcomers had left their homes, it would appear, for reasons ecclesiastical rather than economic and they fell to work in their exile simply to live. The bays, says and frisadoes that comprised the earliest new draperies were made by settlers in the Stour valley on the boarders of Suffolk and Essex, but before long Norwich and Colchester developed as major centres of the manufacture and a range of novel products was being put on offer. As early as c. 1570, the native clothmakers of East Anglia, finding that their usual market was failing them, began after a period of 'necessity and want of living' to imitate the strangers.[10] For a generation or two there was rivalry and even friction to separate the immigrant families from the native textile workers: the disputes turned on such matters as cloth inspection and the tax known as the aulnage, and the strangers were blamed for taking up too much food and accommodation (for aulnage, see page 58). But the manufacture of new draperies percolated steadily westward and northward; by the middle of the seventeenth century they were an established if not dominant component of the English cloth industry. The foreign origins of the new products were not always obvious: thus 'ascots' were simply an anglicised version of the says traditionally made at the Flemish village of Hondschoote.

Many generations were to elapse before the distinction between draperies old and new slipped into oblivion, while broadcloths and kerseys declined into the position of merely two of the immense variety of products offered by the English textile industry. In the marketing of new fabrics, the seventeenth century was an epoch of flexibility and innovation. When in the 1720s Daniel Defoe cast an eye at the products of industry up and down the country, the transformation was still in progress and the fortunes of trade were not uniform. He noted how the manufacture of heavy broadcloths in Kent and at Reading had entered upon a steep decline, while at the ancient textile city of Winchester all clothmaking had come to an end. East Anglia was still the seat of a great textile manufacture: bays were made at Colchester and the nearby market towns, says and perpetuanas at Sudbury, while at Norwich the output of 'stuffs', though damaged by the rivalry of printed calicoes, still continued. Stourbridge Fair, where the varied cloths of the north and west countries were brought for distribution in the domestic market, he compared with the London market itself. Devonshire was prospering on the manufacture of serges, while the backbone of the west country industry was provided by fine medley or Spanish cloths. But if there is any consistent theme underlying the observations of Defoe, it is that that textile market was particularly responsive to the lighter and less expensive products. The fine medley cloths of the west country were being undercut, he remarked, by travelling salesmen from Leeds with their cheaper imitations: Halifax cloths might not be as fine as the Gloucester whites on which they were modelled, but their makers claimed that their colours were as good. It was symptomatic of changing styles of dress that at Devizes the cheap drugget, a material much worn at the time, was displacing traditional broadcloth as the staple product, and that Coventry had turned to the manufacture of tammies while at Newbury and Andover great quantities of shalloons, used for lining men's clothes, were being made. The market was nothing if not competitive and the north was showing signs of drawing ahead.

2 Wool supply and distribution

ENGLISH wool had for centuries been a much-prized commodity in international trade. In mid-thirteenth century it was
being shipped abroad in prodigious quantities, often by Italian
merchants, and it provided the essential raw material also for a
flourishing textile industry in the Netherlands. In the fourteenth century, Edward III had fostered the organisation of the
Company of Merchants of the Staple, a body of English wool-
dealers through whose hands the wool traffic was canalised
with the primary purpose of simplifying the collection of an
export tax to enrich the king's exchequer. From 1363 onwards
the Staplers kept their sales market for foreign buyers – i.e.,
the Staple – at Calais, a fortress in English hands until 1558.
They became increasingly involved in the royal finances and
politics. From 1466, by a special and long-lived arrangement
with the Crown, they took over direct responsibility for the
wages of the garrison at Calais. In the history of English textile
production, the Staplers must inevitably be cast as enemies:
they comprised a rich and influential body of merchants whose
livelihood depended upon whisking abroad the raw material
upon which the English manufacturer had to rely, in order to
sell it at Calais to his rival the Netherlands clothmaker. For
many generations their agents competed with the country
clothier for the goodwill of the country dealers who had fleeces
from the peasant or landowner to sell.

In this competition for English wool the Staplers over the
long term yielded ground. Their annual shipments of wool fell
heavily in the course of the fifteenth century. During the first
decade of the sixteenth, they were steadying around an average
of rather more than six thousand sacks – a sack was reckoned
to hold 365 lb., i.e. the clip from 260 sheep. To these there
should be added a few hundred sacks exported on licence by

Italians who had paid for this privilege. But the decline in the wool export traffic was soon resumed. Customs records indicate that fifty years later the fifteenth-century average had been halved. By the mid-1570s, wool exports seem momentarily to have dried up altogether. The inference is that all the wool available was being wrought into cloth at home: presumably those who had formerly bought up wool for the Staple were finding it easier and no less remunerative to distribute it to the country clothiers, who were being obliged to pay prices that moved higher and higher, particularly for the finest wool. Certainly when in 1578 a delegation from the clothmaking towns of Holland visited England to try to ensure a resumption of the wool trade they met with a cool answer from the Staplers.[11] The English government was more sympathetic and tried, for political if not industrial reasons, to reactivate the wool Staple. But its efforts met with small success. The export of wool, which for the next forty years was no more than an insignificant trickle, was ultimately prohibited from 1614 onwards.[12] But the prohibition, it must be added, was never fully effective. Small amounts of English wool, magnified by rumour and indignation, continued to be 'owled' abroad during the seventeenth and eighteenth centuries despite the vigilance of customs officials.

Thus by the end of the third quarter of the sixteenth century the textile industry had developed sufficiently to absorb virtually all the wool produced within the kingdom. The pundits of the age professed the belief that there were already too many sheep in England, though it was also alleged that the sheep population of the country was if anything a shade smaller than it had been a couple of centuries earlier, when raw wool was being exported in enormous quantities. The situation is not simple to interpret; but it looks as if this was the moment when the English woollen industry had seriously to look overseas for the essential raw material of its products. Irish wool and yarn had long been dribbling through the west coast ports, and there had been minute shipments of wool from Spain and the Baltic, but the importation had not been of significant size. The government in 1552 had tried to restrain wool prices by the enactment of legislation to damp down rural

19

competition for supplies, by forbidding purchases save by Staplers or clothiers.[13] But now in the 1570s the crisis was renewed. In the course of the year 1575 there occurred a sharp increase of unlicenced imports of wool from Spain, following which the government trimmed its sails to meet the situation by encouraging imports from both Spain and the Baltic[14] But since war with Spain was imminent, it is unlikely that much came from this source before the restoration of peace in 1604. Meanwhile, Irish and Polish wool from the Baltic continued to offer the only alternative supplementary sources. Perhaps this shortfall of sheep's wool helps to explain why from the end of the sixteenth century many clothiers in Lancashire tended to change over to making linens, fustians and finally cloths from the cotton wool that was providentially now being shipped direct from the Levant. Thus the overgrown industrial village of Manchester ceased in the course of the seventeenth century to be primarily a seat of the woollen manufacture.

Sheep health fluctuated from year to year and with it the quantity and quality of the annual clip and therefore the price of the wool. Much depended on the portion of the animal from which it had been shorn. In addition, it might be dry or oily, short or long, fine or coarse, clean or dirty, fresh or last season's. But c. 1500 the market basically distinguished wool according to its district of origin. Sheep breeding was localised. Most costly were the fine fleeces from the Welsh Marcher country, fame – and price – attaching particularly to the wool nicknamed 'Leominster ore'; next came the only slightly less valuable Cotswold wool. Middling sorts were produced in Lincolnshire and on the Berkshire Downs, coarse in Suffolk, Sussex and elsewhere, though the really cheap wool originated in the north country and Cornwall.[15] The clothier, whose function was to organise cloth manufacture and marketing, may sometimes have bought his supplies direct from the sheep-owners, but the evidence suggests that he often relied for his purchases upon a middleman, sometimes a wayward Stapler who in the sixteenth century braved the hostility of the law to 'regraters' who bought only to sell again, and to 'engrossers' who hoarded in expectation of a price rise. These middlemen were the ubiquitous wool brokers or 'broggers' often denounced by those who resented the general tendency of prices to rise, though this in all likelihood was due more to the competition of buyers for supplies. In fact, the wool middleman performed an essential economic function as a distributor, transporting the raw material of the manufacturer from often remote country pastures to the industrialised regions.

Certainly the wool-brogger was disliked by the large-scale clothier, which helps to explain why there was legislation in 1489, 1531, 1546 and 1552 designed to fortify the law by curbing all sales of wool by the grower save to Staplers or clothmakers.[16] But the services of the brogger were appreciated by the smaller producers. It was to appease the humble spinners of Norfolk that in 1547 a statute was enacted to enable them to buy their dribblets of wool from middlemen; and in 1555 the cottagers of the moorland parish of Halifax, too poor to keep a horse to carry wool from the market-place, were similarly permitted to buy from the itinerant 'wool-driver', as he was called in Yorkshire.[17] Such traffickers were on the increase during the sixteenth century: a government enquiry in 1577 revealed widespread activity on the part of wool middlemen, from well-known Staplers to insignificant broggers, and over large parts of the country.[18] Such intermediaries did not merely relieve the poor spinner or weaver from trudging to the market to fetch his raw materials; they also contributed to his needs by sorting and redistributing the wool to suit local requirements. As time passed it may be that the sheep-master tended to look more to butchers and tanners rather than wool-buyers for his profits and yet, as there was an increasingly complex variety of cloths being manufactured, each with its own specialised requirements, the intervention of a middleman was more useful than ever. By the middle of the seventeenth century the Staplers, their exporting activities now a dim memory, were defending themselves by pointing to their essential services to both wool-grower and clothmaker, between whom they claimed to provide an essential channel, greased as necessary by credit.[19] The wool dealer had come to stay.

Closer inspection suggests how miscellaneous were the routes along which supplies of wool might pass from the back of the sheep to the loom of the manufacturer. The Isham brothers, City merchants who traded in cloths at Antwerp in mid-sixteenth century, accumulated wool at their Northamptonshire estates for disposal to clothiers whose products they did not always buy. A couple of generations later, there were enterprising middlemen, particularly in the west country, who organised the spinning of their wool into yarn before offering it on the market. The large-scale import of Spanish wool from the early seventeenth century onwards was perhaps some encouragement to these 'yarn badgers' or 'market spinners' who also served the growing demand for coloured cloths by anticipating the clothiers and dyeing their wool before it was spun. Since coloured 'Spanish' cloths proved much in demand, there were soon imitations in which English wool replaced wholly or in part the expensive raw material. 'Medley cloths', dyed in the wool, were prominent in the west country output from mid-seventeenth century. The yarn distributed by yarn badgers was distrusted by many clothiers because, being pieced together from different sources, it was uneven in quality; nevertheless, ready-made yarn as well as wool was being imported from Ireland from the late seventeenth century and perhaps earlier. No doubt the yarn badger, by tapping the labour of rural districts that lacked a cloth industry, was meeting a real need. In the eighteenth century, wool was sometimes dispensed to clothiers through the agency of Blackwell Hall factors (see page 42).

3 Industrial organisation and location

THE entrepreneur who organised the market for the manual worker at his loom was known during the sixteenth century in southern England, including East Anglia, as the clothman or clothier. Increasingly often he delivered the yarn to the weaver and perhaps also owned it. He might well have owned the wool even before it had passed over the spinning-wheel. But his crucial responsibility lay in the delivery of the cloth to the London market and finding a purchaser there. In good times he might find his reward in the accumulation of profit, in bad times he risked bankruptcy or otherwise going to the wall. The details of organisation were never clear-cut nor uniform and varied greatly in time and place. At the moment when the independent Halifax weaver was trudging to the local market to sell his cloths, the weaver of the west country was more accustomed to deliver his to his neighbour the clothman, who might seem little more than a glorified carrier. But if the neighbour also took the opportunity to consign yarn for the next batch of cloths, and entered into any sort of contract or even understanding with the weaver, then their relationship was evidently edging towards that of employer and employee – especially if it were recognised that yarn and subsequently cloth alike belonged to the clothier, as he was increasingly called, to the exclusion of the old-fashion term 'clothman'. In the north country, it was the weaver who often answered to the description of 'clothier', the purchaser of his cloths at Leeds and other market towns being the 'merchant'. When the weavers of north Wales brought their 'cottons' and 'friezes' (both woven from woollen yarn) to the market at Oswestry, they were bought by the 'drapers' of Shrewsbury, whose role was the parallel one of organisation. But elsewhere, when the industry centred directly on the London market, the terminology was uniform: the craftsmen who manufactured the cloth remained weavers, fullers and so forth; the organisers of manufacture were 'clothiers'; and the description of merchant was reserved for the Londoners who bought the cloths for resale, often abroad.

At the place of manufacture, the relationship between clothier and weaver does not admit of any simple description. To equate them with employer and employee, as these were known after the advent of the industrial revolution, would be misleading, if only because either party might be only a part-time participant, and the weaver might and often did serve more than one master. In early seventeenth-century Gloucestershire, a major seat of the broadcloth industry, there were 1 700 woollen weavers whose output was ultimately destined in large part for the London market. The transport of the cloths to Blackwell Hall, it is to be assumed, was the business of the 200 or so individuals described as clothiers who lived among them. Some of these clothiers undoubtedly were well-off propertied men, but most of them can have differed little in economic or social status from their neighbours the purely manual workers. Some clothiers, perhaps most, themselves worked at the loom. Most, indeed, kept no servant or apprentice in attendance, while about one in twenty of the weavers lived in sufficient style to do so. The willingness of the clothier to confront the market – his distinctive service – clearly by itself brought him no social advancement. It involved personal labour, the use of judgement and the acceptance of serious risk, for which there was a reward in any resultant profit. The large-scale industrialist, though he may well have often controlled a significant share of the output of cloths, comprised always a small minority among the clothiers. In Manchester, at about the same time, the woollen cloth market was dominated by the Mosleys and a handful of related families, though aulnage was also paid (and ownership of cloths thereby implied) by a whole crowd of small men, some of them described as 'shearmen' and others with non-textile interests.[20]

As far as the evidence goes, the heyday of the large-scale clothier, famous even outside his own county, fell within the three or four generations before the overthrow of the

Merchants Adventurers in 1614. Jack of Newbury, William Stumpe of Malmesbury, Peter Blundell of Tiverton and Randall Tench of Leeds were all known if not to the monarch personally (as more than one of them was) then at least to some chief councillors of the sovereign. They had characters sufficiently colourful to leave a memory of their deeds behind them. There were few textile industrialists of comparable fame in the later seventeenth and eighteenth centuries – why, we can only speculate. It may be that the new draperies were less readily adaptable to large-scale organisation than the more standardised old draperies.[21] Perhaps the existence of a more or less unified foreign market at Antwerp had simplified the making of business contacts and so the building of a large-scale concern. Conceivably the more violent trade oscillations of the sixteenth century favoured the capable clothier, who possessed the exceptional ability to ride out the occasional storms. Just possibly it is a matter of perspective: in the sixteenth century the cloth manufacture and trade were virtually alone in offering a business pathway to riches, while in the course of the seventeenth century additional openings in mining and manufacture were becoming available, so that the spotlight fell less upon clothiers. Of course, there was no lack of sizeable firms in the eighteenth century. Indeed, it was believed that conditions for the small man had deteriorated during the seventeenth century in the west country, and the initial capital required for starting a business using Spanish wool is said to have risen from £300 to £500 in the hundred years to 1750. But this did not inhibit the development of large firms; and when the few oak trees have multiplied into a forest they individually attract less attention.

As to the clothworkers who finished the broadcloths in early seventeenth-century Gloucestershire, they usually ran their own workshops, some with their own servants. We know that the wealthiest clothiers actually retained in their own employment, i.e. for regular wages, some of the fullers, tuckers, shearers, dyers and other craftsmen whose skill was needed to transform the rough fabric straight from the loom into the fine smooth cloth required by the ultimate consumer. But even if the clothworker retained his independence of any employer and worked on commission for various clothiers, weavers or others, he was seldom or never a figure of much consequence. Thus in the expanding industry of the West Riding of Yorkshire in the eighteenth century, the fuller usually leased his mill from the landlord who owned it. Fulling-mills were valued variously at from £50 to £150, but to find the money to pay for the use of this piece of fixed capital the fuller had to ply his trades of shearing and fulling, for which he was paid by the piece by the neighbouring clothiers. The beneficiary was the mill-owner, often a landed gentleman, but sometimes described as 'yeoman', 'tanner' or even 'grocer'. The fuller's most valuable equipment was likely to be his shears, if indeed he owned them; but many were also part-time farmers.[22]

The industrial organisation prevailing in early seventeenth-century Gloucestershire, as elsewhere, was that known today as the domestic or putting-out system and which was generally prevalent throughout the English woollen textile industry during the quarter-millennium with which we are concerned. Spinner and weaver alike worked at home, in hours of their own choice, whatever their arrangements with the clothier. Between the workman and his organiser there prevailed a rough social equilibrium, though there were always possibilities of friction. Clothiers might suspect their weavers of embezzling scraps of the yarn committed to them, or of producing deceitful or otherwise unsatisfactory cloths, while weavers might resent over-close attempts at regulation or to force down their wages, or otherwise meet the dulness of the market. There is circumstantial evidence of rudimentary labour organisation to defend wage-levels in seventeenth-century Wiltshire; in the next century there were also stirrings in Gloucestershire and Devon, as also in the West Riding and perhaps elsewhere. But the information is thin or one-sided because of the hostility of the law to industrial combination.[23] Other problems and innovations were also provoked by the ups and downs of trade. Thus in the mid-sixteenth century when market demand momentarily seemed insatiable some enterprising west country clothiers, notably William Stumpe of Malmesbury, thought to supervise their weavers – presumably recently recruited – by assembling them to work together in disused monastic buildings serving for the occasion as weaving-sheds. Such experiments were few and short-lived, and they collapsed when the market recovered from its fever.

As to the actual level of earnings, little is to be fruitfully established in the context of the woollen industry by itself. It is misleading to project backwards the hard-and-fast relation-ships of employer and employee as they crystallised in the nineteenth century; the essential unit of production was usually the family, where much labour, paid or unpaid, was contributed by female hands, while outside the urban areas the men often had an acre or two to cultivate, perhaps particularly in the earlier period. It is evident that the textile industry was labour-intensive, particularly where coarse or undyed cloths were concerned. The implements used in it were cheap and easily constructed, even broad looms being valued at no more than a matter of shillings, though a dye-house or a set of shearman's tools represented a larger outlay. It was reckoned by the lawyer Sir Matthew Hale in the later seventeenth century that of the costs of making 'a common coarse medley cloth', the wages of the various craftsmen contributed just over half, while the wool itself absorbed only 38 per cent. No doubt for the costly cloths the fine wool was more expensive and absorbed more; Hale's younger contemporary the Wiltshire clothier George Wansey paid twice as much for the Spanish wool he bought as Hale's Gloucestershire clothier had for his wool, but he may well have had to give higher wages for the more exacting labour involved. So pronounced a dependence upon the human element made the industry almost as sensitive to the hazards of weather and health as agriculture, to which it was indivisibly bound. But the payment of labour was not left entirely to chance or the blind operation of market forces. For most of the time, the government also had an eye on it, though the regulation of wages under the Statute of Artificers of 1563 offered a dangerously frail bulwark for the well-being of a community in moments of stress. But so hazy and variable were the frontiers of social need that it would be rash to attempt to define precisely the overall movement of real wages. Any realistic evaluation of remuneration of labour involves a full

27

consideration of the social structure, the prevalence of part-time occupations, payment by piece-work and the provision of meat and drink with wages.[24]

Indeed, neither weaver nor clothier should be regarded as invariably dependent upon the textile industry for a living, particularly in the sixteenth and seventeenth centuries. The old draperies in their heyday were to an unknown but not insignificant extent the products of a peasant workforce that turned to the loom when the seasons for ploughing and reaping had passed. When in the 1530s John Leland passed through a string of what he called 'pretty clothing towns' (i.e., villages in the modern sense) in the open-field regions of the west country, he must have taken it for granted that the copyholders and the makers of cloths were identical, though the opportunities for clothmaking in the enclosed dairy-farming districts were perhaps even greater. The yeoman-clothiers of the early seventeenth century who dwelt in the hills beside the Colne valley in the West Riding had a counter-part in the farmer-weavers who flourished in the vale country of the north-west Wiltshire Avon or beside Stroudwater in Gloucestershire. Textile workers during the sixteenth century and even later often had their own small holdings in the fields, or at least the right to pasture their beasts on the commons. But it is a reasonable conjecture – evidence has not yet been fully marshalled – that the immigrants who planted the new draperies were harbingers of change. They were urbanised specialists opening by their very presence a road to further change and refinement. So it is to be suspected that the connection with the land became less intimate in the century before 1750; but an account of the multiplication of the full-time or professional craftsman has yet to be written.

Admittedly, however much the industry may be considered a rural phenomenon, there were always some important urban seats of woollen manufacture. As textile centres, the ancient cities of Lincoln and Coventry were by the sixteenth century far gone in decline, and York and even Salisbury were following in their wake. But there were new points of development, the most remarkable of which was the venerable city of Worcester. Thanks to the Severn, it was well served by its communications, and in addition it was conveniently situated close to the finest wool-producing districts of Hereford and Shropshire. Its potential rival as the local textile metropolis was Hereford, whose corporation sacrificed the advantage of a favourable location by some clumsy politics in the reign of Henry VII. Its fulling-mills were 'thrown down and destroyed' in 1527, and the city was thereafter bereft of industry.[25] Worcester was able to promote a special Act of Parliament in 1533 designed to stifle rural clothmaking in the surrounding countryside, and it acquired a charter of incorporation in 1555 with wide powers of self-government. Worcester cloths had already won a reputation in the export market, and the new corporation was dominated by clothiers who were soon exerting themselves to increase it. This they aimed to do by the enforcement of a full apprenticeship upon textile workers and by insisting upon a systematic inspection of their products – a policy that produced perhaps the closest English approximation to a continental clothmaking town after the fashion of Florence or Ypres. Worcester was the home of skilled and urbanised weavers, who had lost touch with the land and bought their food in the market. Their fine broadcloths were famous far and wide, until late in the seventeenth century when the market developed other tastes and the industry went downhill.

There were other comparable clothmaking centres at this time in England. One such was the clothmaking and finishing centre of Leeds in the West Riding of Yorkshire, where at an interval of two or three generations a similar course was being pursued. Leeds was not a historic centre like Worcester, but an industrialised village in a lower Pennine valley, with the added advantage of being near to the Humberside port of Hull. Leeds achieved its grant of incorporation in 1626, and its new rulers were led by a vigorous group of clothiers, whose successors proved no less resolute than their Worcester counterparts. Norwich and Colchester might be cited as yet other examples of urban clothmaking towns. The market town of Reading too was long renowned for its kerseys, though the local records that might illuminate its history have perished. Of course, there was no lack of English villages where clothmaking and consequent industrialisation led to a rapid growth of population and a

29

quasi-urban nucleus from the fifteenth century, as for instance Lavenham and Long Melford in Suffolk, Manchester in Lancashire or Trowbridge and Castle Combe in Wiltshire. Early sixteenth-century Lavenham stood momentarily as high as the thirteenth place in taxable wealth among provincial towns, just above York and Totnes, thanks no doubt to the residence of the wealthy clothier Thomas Spring and the many workers dependent upon him.[26] But such places did not enjoy the administrative autonomy of a borough, nor the spirit that appropriately matched the issue of a charter, and fell within the jurisdiction of the country justices. They remained just fragments of the county that, for better or worse, happened to have become to some extent industrialised if not urbanised.

Thus intensive textile activity while frequently rural was far from entirely so. Clothmaking was ubiquitous. It is however practicable to point to certain regions where it was concentrated, and where the output was often destined for an overseas market. The prime broadcloth-making region in the sixteenth and seventeenth centuries lay in the west country, beside the streams flowing from the Cotswolds and Mendips, i.e. within the counties of Gloucester, Oxford, Wiltshire and Somerset. East Anglia, particularly Suffolk, was also a major site of textile production, specialising in broadcloth manufacture until this was replaced by the new draperies of the immigrants late in the sixteenth century. A smaller broadcloth-making district lay in southern Kent, centering on Cranbrook, until it died out in the later seventeenth century. Broadcloths were certainly made elsewhere, but the main product of the very important textile-producing regions in Devonshire and the West Riding at this time was kerseys or at least cloths of the kersey type. There is no simple explanation of why the spectacular woollen industry of the early modern period should thus have been localised. Possibly the availability of a supply of fine wool nearby, as at Worcester, gave some encouragement. The presence of streams to provide water power for fulling-mills also may have helped. Perhaps the diversity of manorial customs was relevant: a historian of Yorkshire has pointed out how the tenants of land in 'ancient demesne' were more lightly burdened by seigneurial demands than their neighbours: they could therefore more readily set aside a stock of wool to make cloth for the market.[27] Food supply was another consideration: where partible inheritance was customary, as in the Leicestershire countryside, knitting provided a means to compensate for the holding that grew smaller with every new generation. Likewise in the seventeenth century, smallholders in the Forest of Arden took to the making of cloths to pay for the provisions supplied by their farming neighbours.[28]

II Marketing

4 Who wore English cloth?

CLOTHMAKING was an occupation almost as ubiquitous as baking and brewing: weaving perhaps only a little less, spinning rather more so. A variable proportion of the output, up to half or sometimes even more, of English textiles was destined for wear at home. Local homespun cloth continued after, as before, 1500 to be worn in the family and in the village, though some pieces might pass to a buyer at the nearby fair or market town. Others were carried further afield. The national market for textiles was served by various major fairs, of which the most frequented were Bartholomew Fair at Smithfield in the City each August, and Stourbridge Fair held near Cambridge. Most important of all by far was the weekly cloth market open from Thursday to Saturday in London at Blackwell Hall. At these and other times and places, the cloths continued to change hands: there were indeed innumerable occasions when they might pass from the hands of the manufacturer or entrepreneur who organised manufacture, but here our attention must be confined to those most usual for the vendor. In the west country, when weavers and some other textile workers were often tethered to agriculture for at least the seasons of ploughing and harvesting, there were in the early sixteenth century a few clothmakers seemingly content to entrust their broadcloths to the local carrier to be transported to the London market and sold for what they might fetch. But as industrial organisation developed, it became the special responsibility of the clothier to ride to the City and bargain in

32

person at Blackwell Hall with the merchant, whether a draper supplying the home market or an exporter. There was a well-organised domestic distribution network by which cloths and other wares – books, for example – were conveyed from London to the provinces: not for nothing was there a specially close relationship in the later sixteenth century between the Drapers' and Stationers' Companies of the City of London.[29]

Who were the cloth-dealers who purchased cloths for export from the country clothier at Blackwell Hall? In the sixteenth century they were chiefly Londoners who belonged to the Company of Merchants Adventurers, a privileged body with monopoly rights over English trade with the Netherlands. Before 1552, the countryman might also meet Germans belonging to one or another of the cities of the Hanseatic League, who enjoyed special rights from both the English Crown and the City. There were also the southern merchants resident at London, whether Italians, Spaniards or Ragusans, whose activities were somewhat pruned by an Act of Parliament in 1523.[30] But whoever the buyer might be, he was someone experienced in ways of business overseas. By the mid-eighteenth century, the scene had completely changed. Clothier and merchant had lost contact. Separating them there had appeared an intermediary, the Blackwell Hall factor, to whose warehouse the goods from the country might well be regularly consigned. It was his business to store them for distribution to the appropriate exporter, or to the draper for the home market. Both clothier and purchaser were now more sedentary in their business habits. The market was probably more cut-and-dried in its practices than it had been a couple of centuries earlier, with long-term contracts, invoices and samples playing a larger part, though even in the early sixteenth century the conditions of sale were carefully defined in the bargain, and the clothier supplied 'skantlyns or examples' of the cloths to be delivered.[31]

The essential importance of the protected home market for English cloths need not be doubted, though only stray scraps of information come to hand about it. We learn that in sixteenth-century Worcester the woollen cloths woven on the narrow loom were for domestic consumption, while the broadcloths went for export; and in 1591 it was reported from the West Riding of Yorkshire how the best Wakefield cloths and certain other types were not usually exported abroad but 'worn within the realm'.[32] It was from the home market that much of the welcome for the new draperies in the seventeenth century was derived. But to suggest what proportions of the total output were consumed respectively at home and abroad is difficult. Presumably the domestic market grew roughly in step with the rise in population, which is believed to have doubled, more or less, in the century before 1640, after which the rate of increase was more gentle; and at times of buoyant foreign trade the proportion of exports is likely to have grown. In 1621, at a moment therefore of marked depression in foreign trade, an observer hazarded that not quite 40 per cent of the cloth output was transported abroad.[33] A modern analyst has suggested that in the eighteenth century the share of exports rose from two-fifths to at least two-thirds.[34] It may well be that, for example, at times in the middle decades of the sixteenth century, during the heyday of the Antwerp mart, as much as two-thirds of the total output of woollen cloths was being shipped overseas. In fact we are in the dark.[35] But it was usually the repercussions of the regular dispatch of a spectacularly vast quantity of textiles to overseas markets that gripped the attention of contemporaries, raising problems of international, political, social and economic significance; and hence it is with exports that this essay must chiefly be concerned.

Englishmen were always reluctant to accept that their woollen cloths were not articles suitable for universal consumption. There was undoubtedly a natural market on their doorstep among the inhabitants of the wind-swept plains of northern Europe and of the mountainous peninsulas further south that stretched from Pyrenees, Alps and Carpathians into the Mediterranean, with their chilly winters: further afield, the warmth of the climate removed the attractions of such heavy textiles. Hence it was that from the later middle ages onwards Germany and the adjacent lands of central Europe provided a welcoming market for the fine cloths produced in the Netherlands and England. Netherlands cloths owed their qualities to the wool from which they too were made, i.e. the

34

best English fleeces, as supplied to continental manufacturers chiefly by the Staplers at their Calais mart. This was why in Germany *c*. 1500 the woollen cloths from the north-west, whether woven on Netherlands or English looms, were known indiscriminately as *panni pulchri*, the handsome cloths. For many generations the major suppliers of these textiles were the clothmakers of Flanders and Brabant, but in the fifteenth century the products of the northerly province of Holland and of England itself came to the fore. In the sixteenth century, as deliveries of wool by the Staplers dwindled more and more, English cloths increasingly dominated the market. But already by *c*. 1500 English cloths were being sold in the upper Rhine valley, Alsace and even Switzerland, while eastwards they had percolated beyond Vienna to Hungary and Transylvania. Some were being carried over the Alps by the merchants of Cologne for sale at Venice and beyond, thereby reaching a southern region that was also supplied by sea, chiefly by Italian and Ragusan merchants.[36]

English cloths were thus enjoying a widespread market abroad even before the end of the middle ages because in quality they had few rivals. There was plentiful production of middling quality and coarse cloths in the Rhineland; but the establishment of a textile industry manufacturing really fine cloth was hindered by the unsettled condition of the German countryside. Nor was suitable wool readily at hand. However, there were well-off knights and townsfolk in number sufficient to provide a market.[37] As to the general situation in the early 1560s, we happen to be informed by the reply of the Merchants Adventurers to an enquiry by the Privy Council. This elicited the information that West Country and Kentish undyed broad-cloths were believed to be mostly 'spent and consumed' in Germany and the Netherlands. Coloured broadcloths, of which only relatively small quantities were exported, were for sale in peripheral regions from Poland in the north to Spain, Portugal and Barbary in the south. Kerseys had a market in Germany and the Netherlands also, though northern and Hampshire kerseys were additionally consumed in Hungary, Italy, southern Europe and the Levant. France took little more than some Devonshire kerseys, chiefly the coarser types; the finest were wanted in Spain, whence many were shipped across the Atlantic to the New World.[38] But all in all, it was evidently the accepted belief that most consumers of English woollen textiles shipped abroad lived in central Europe, whether north or south of the Alps. The gateway to this region was the universal entrepôt of Antwerp, now at the zenith of its brilliance.

Despite many minor variations in pattern, the ultimate destination of English woollen cloths abroad remained much the same in the first half of the eighteenth century as it had been 200 or more years earlier, though the approaches to it had been radically altered. The universal gateway of Antwerp had long been replaced by a score of lesser havens of entry; but the consumers remained preponderantly western Europeans, whatever region of the continent they inhabited. With the world-wide commerce opened up in the seventeenth century and fostered by the Acts of Trade and other mercantile legislation, the woollen industry had little direct contact. Thus according to the customs records for the year 1750, the end of the period covered in this survey, and at the opening of an interval of general peace, it was to continental Europe that 67 per cent of the miscellaneous short and long cloths, 79 per cent of the 'Spanish' cloths and 82 per cent of the men's worsted stockings exported were shipped. Among the more recently-developed manufactures, for flannels the proportion was 73 per cent and for 'stuffs' 80 per cent. For the most widely-made 'new draperies', i.e. serges and perpetuanas, it was 94 per cent. There was however a threat lurking behind the persistence of the ancient continental market. Its constituent portions varied in their absorbtion of English textiles; but by and large it was somewhat stagnant during the first half of the eighteenth century, consuming only a little more in 1750 than it had done before the outbreak of the War of the Spanish Succession fifty years earlier. The dynamic market that ultimately enabled the English woollen industry to survive the operation of Napoleon's 'Continental System' lay in North America. But the major development of the direct transatlantic colonial market for woollen textiles came only in the later eighteenth century.

Meanwhile, the cloth trade always had trials to face in its struggle to retain more than a foothold in the continental market. There were trade recessions during the years of war, which discouraged the commodity traffic; but the restoration of peace sometimes meant, as in some German states after 1648, the erection of barriers to textiles of foreign make. The thawing of Anglo-French relations in the later sixteenth century, which enabled a market for Devonshire kerseys and Welsh friezes and 'cottons' to develop at Rouen, was reversed in the course of the seventeenth and ended with the protectionist measures of Colbert; a revival of the French market had to await the conclusion of the Eden free trade treaty of 1786. However, as late as the fiscal year 1668–9, as much as 70 per cent of the 'Spanish' broadcloths shipped from London was destined for Germany either direct or through the Netherlands. Later, the long-established trade to Hamburg was said to be damaged by the encouragement of the linen industry in Scotland and Ireland, which was a deterrent to the import of German linens. Russia, Poland and the Baltic, which in the very late sixteenth and early seventeenth centuries had seemed to offer very promising outlets, subsequently took very little and were regarded as 'the lost trades', though something was regained by the Anglo-Russian agreement of 1734. However, the share of Spain and Portugal in the continental market grew. Already in the 1660s the Peninsula took from 8.7 per cent to 13.6 per cent of the export of 'Spanish' cloths. In the early eighteenth century, the import of Spanish wool and with it the manufacture of 'Spanish' cloths was inevitably constricted by the War of the Spanish Succession; but in general the Peninsular cloth market was sufficiently buoyant in the first half of the eighteenth century to offset setbacks in countries further to the east. An unknown proportion of the cloths shipped to the Peninsula ultimately made their way to consumers in Latin America.

It may be that there was a slight southward shift in the consumption of English woollens, though in the year 1715, when peace had been firmly restored and the export of 'Spanish' cloths was once more flourishing, 62 per cent of them still went to northern and central Europe, and 33 per cent to southern. But there is no doubt that the ancient Venetian woollen industry came to grief in the early seventeenth century owing to Dutch and English competition, the final blow being a redirection of the Spanish wool export route from Alicante and the Mediterranean to Bilbao and the north Atlantic in the 1630s: the looms of Venice were ultimately starved of their raw material.[39] But it must be recalled that English cloths were at this time no novelty in Mediterranean lands, where in the sixteenth century kerseys were widely consumed. In the early decades from c. 1500, English cloths made their way through the Straits of Gibraltar in ships of Ragusa or of Venice or Genoa, and a few were even carried in English bottoms.[40] But in addition, perhaps most were making their way southwards overland along the well-organised trans-continental route over the Alps, until the abrupt severance of friendly relations with the governments of the Netherlands and Spain in 1569, which for practical purposes put an end to the Antwerp entrepôt. The Ragusan traffic was at its peak in the years 1515–35, over 26,000 kerseys being brought in 1531 to Ragusa whence they were distributed throughout the Ottoman empire.[41] There is no means of measuring the quantity of English textiles passing southwards in the sixteenth century, whether overland or by sea. It may not have been strikingly less than the 20 or 30 per cent of English textile exports (varying according to the method of computation) carried by sea in English ships to Italy and the Levant in the first half of the eighteenth century. But the agents of distribution were new. The Ragusans and Italians of the earlier epoch had been replaced by City firms and the English Levant Company.

5 The wholesale market and its mechanisms

THE manufacture of cloth was an occupation widely scattered throughout England, and English textiles were dispersed over a large area of the adjacent continent as well as at home. In contrast to this the wholesale market for cloths consumed both at home and abroad was always to a high degree concentrated at London, the nodal point for internal communications since the Roman occupation. Besides, the shortest and most convenient line of access for the transport of cloths lay from the mouth of the Thames to the Rhine delta, along a trade route that by 1500 was already long established and organised. Thus the nerve-centre of the cloth trade on the English side was inevitably sited at London, where in the first decade of the sixteenth century at least 61 per cent of the cloth exports of England was being shipped. A generation later, in the decade 1534–44, this proportion had swollen to over 84 per cent and was soon to increase. In the fiscal year 1568–9 as much as 93 per cent of the cloth customs duty was collected at London.[42] There were fluctuations and a long-term tendency for the over-whelming preponderance of the City to recede. But it has been estimated that in the first forty years of the seventeenth century about three quarters of the total woollen textile exports still passed through London despite some loss of West Riding trade to Hull and despite the opening of a trade in Devonshire cloths direct from Exeter to the Netherlands which provoked some resentment in the City. In the fiscal year 1676–7, 72 per cent of the whole customs revenue was still being drawn from the port of London. Only in the middle decades of the eighteenth century did the share of London in the export of English products – of which woollen goods in the 1730s were providing some 78 per cent in value – wobble and begin to drop below two thirds. Few cloths were actually made in London; but it

39

was in the City that the national cloth market was always located.

The site of the market was from 1397 the building or congeries of buildings near the Guildhall, in Basinghall Street, known as Blackwell Hall. The City was insistent that all cloths should be sold there and nowhere else, the purpose being to retain all the dealings with the country manufacturers in the hands of citizens of London. A small fee was levied at the sale of each cloth, and also on cloths remaining on the premises unsold after a certain lapse of time, so that the market generated an appreciable revenue, to the benefit of the City or its agents. The right to nominate the Keeper of Blackwell Hall was for many years a privilege of the Drapers' Company; but ultimately in 1557 the management of the market, with the collection and receipt of the fees, was handed over as an endowment to Christ's Hospital. The Keeper was aided in enforcing market regulations by a staff of clerks and porters; his administration was inspected by occasionally appointed surveyors, until in mid-seventeenth century a permanent supervisory committee came into existence at the Guildhall. The cloth market at Blackwell Hall functioned for over four centuries. In its busiest days it was one of the major commodity markets of the world, second only, perhaps, to the Old Bourse at Antwerp. Despite various setbacks, the turnover of cloths was generally on the increase; no doubt it was because of the pressure on space that the whole market was in 1588 rebuilt as 'a new, strong and beautiful storehouse'.[43] Within its precincts were various specialised salerooms where particular varieties of English textiles were on offer – there was the Spanish Hall, the Bay Hall, the Worcester Hall, the Colchester and Suffolk Hall and so forth. The bustle, the salesmanship, the fraud and the tensions of this marketplace have passed unrecorded. The use of Blackwell Hall began seriously to decline in the second quarter of the eighteenth century, and the market closed down early in the nineteenth.

Country clothiers and City merchants necessarily pursued their joint concerns in close relationship with each other, though not always in full agreement. Londoners always resented the competition of foreign merchants, while the country people welcomed it, though they were disconcerted by the tendency of Italian cloth-buyers to substitute paper for cash in payment. A far-reaching statute regulating the Blackwell Hall market was enacted in 1523.[44] It bears signs of compromise between the clothmaking interest and the London merchants. It established and also limited the rights of foreign merchants, who might buy cloths at Blackwell Hall but only after a lapse of eight days from their delivery for sale to the market. Further, they were enjoined to pay for their purchases in ready money or goods within a month. The act also endorsed the contention of the merchants, already voiced in 1518, that cloths sent up to London in fulfilment of country-made bargains need not be brought to Blackwell Hall but might be consigned direct to the warehouse of the purchaser;[45] and despite the opening for evasion of City regulations offered by this loophole the point was in the next generation accepted by Christ's Hospital. Later still, 'out clerks' were appointed to collect the hallage fee due on cloths delivered by contract direct to private addresses.[46] There is no doubt that enterprising merchants did seek to establish contact with the clothiers in the country: the merchant adventurer John Isham was prepared to ride north to Yorkshire in the 1560s and offer his West Riding clothmakers freshly-minted coins and even silver spoons, to spur them to be punctual in deliveries. The privileged Germans of the Hanse Steelyard as well as the Merchants Adventurers sometimes concluded bargains in the country with the manufacturer, and they enjoyed some reputation for prompt payments. But their share in cloth exports from London was a fluctuating one, with a somewhat declining trend. The fiscal year 1504–5 was the last occasion on which they actually shipped more cloths than their English rivals, their share of London exports momentarily reaching 42 per cent as against the Englishmens' 40 per cent. The remaining 18 per cent fell to other foreigners, probably mainly southern merchants.

No doubt the country clothier regretted the absence of the Hanse merchants from 1552, when their privileges were withdrawn by the Crown and they lost their right of access to Blackwell Hall. The other foreign merchants were also squeezed out of business to some extent in subsequent years, so that the predominance of the Merchants Adventurers became more marked than ever. But their triumph was short-lived. In the first few days of 1569 there occurred a brusque rupture of the traffic to Antwerp, which was never fully resumed; the universal entrepôt at Antwerp in the course of the next decade or so was itself brought to ruin. Consequently, in the final third of the sixteenth century, English cloths had to find new routes to their habitual customers on the continent; these led through half-a-dozen or more ports of entry all around the coasts of Europe instead of passing through the one familiar easy gateway. For instance, from the 1570s onwards, broadcloths and kerseys were being shipped direct to the Baltic and the Mediterranean. The Merchants Adventurers themselves ultimately found a new headquarters at Hamburg. They also strove to continue their traffic with one or another port in the Netherlands, but in the course of two or three generations their business there was undermined by interlopers who could not be constrained to respect their monopoly in law, in addition to other weaknesses. Thus by the early seventeenth century the cloth merchants of the City had lost their singleness of purpose and were fragmented into various interest groups trading to different portions of the European coast, some in chartered monopoly companies, but increasingly many not. The cloth trade was also more complicated because of the rise of the new draperies, which brought with it a transformation in the variety of textiles available for consumption, whether at home or abroad.

It was under these circumstances, when the immediate interests of the merchants were more and more dispersed and the variety of the cloths they sought to market was ever-increasing, that there rose to prominence a new type of middleman, the Blackwell Hall factor, whose advent has already been mentioned.[47] His function was to impose some sort of organisation upon the otherwise chaotic central market by buying goods from the clothier, seeing to their quality and storage as necessary, and finally locating the merchant who might serve the appropriate purchaser abroad. In addition, the Blackwell Hall factors often came to supply credit, to pass on complaints and advice, and even to help in providing a stock of wool. The rise of these middlemen was a gradual process which might be traced back to the sixteenth century. They came to the fore particularly at moments of a market stoppage, when country clothiers met with difficulty in disposing of their goods. The factors offered to pack, store and even advance a little money on the unsold cloths. Since some of them at least were clothworkers by occupation and therefore accustomed to handle goods delivered from the country, their activity might not seem to be much of an innovation. But a number of interests were alarmed, and in the early seventeenth century the City bestirred itself about complaints of unauthorised buying and selling. The trade crisis of 1621–2 was marked by renewed outcries, the drapers denouncing 'certain irregular persons called packing clothworkers and other mean people' who bargained and made contracts, often with foreigners, in their private warehouses. They were alleged to carry patterns in their pockets, to show to both foreigners and 'country chapmen', thereby cutting out the drapers.[48] But since the Blackwell Hall factors were meeting a genuine need the City could do no more than hamper their emergence.

It was only in the later seventeenth century that the Blackwell Hall factors came to dominate the market. A few were grudgingly licenced by the City to operate in the 1660s, and from 1676–8 they were enabled to rent warehouses within the precincts of the Hall from Christ's Hospital. Incidentally but inevitably, the country clothier was henceforth cut off from any direct contact with the exporting merchant. Cloth manufacturers resented the supremacy of these new intermediaries, at least at first, and complained of their dictatorial habits and of the oppressive bargains they drove. They envied them for their wealth. Particularly to the small clothier, their slowness in payment seemed oppressive. These resentments found vent in an Act of Parliament of 1697 which gave statutory authority to the existing regulations of the cloth market and thereby applied some indirect check to the Blackwell Hall factors.[49] But the significance of the act lay less in any effect it may have had upon the cloth trade than in offering a demonstration of the political influence of the country clothiers in parliamentary constituencies within industrial regions. The Blackwell Hall factors provided a directing authority for the woollen textile industry throughout the eighteenth century, save for the relatively small quantities of cloths shipped at the outports, particularly Hull, where they were bought and sorted by the 'gentlemen merchants' of Leeds. For the parties concerned, the Blackwell Hall factors simplified the selection of wares and the choice of markets.

6 The searching of cloths

CLOTHS after leaving the cottage of the weaver were the subject of up to half-a-dozen transactions between successive merchants and might travel hundreds of miles before reaching their ultimate consumer perhaps far in the interior of the continent, the itinerary taking some months. At its end, cloths were sometimes found to be imperfect in one way or another – lacking in size or weight, uneven in texture, disfigured by holes, or overstretched so that they shrank when wet. How was the distant wearer to bring home these defects to the manufacturer? One answer to the problem lay in the efficacy of the open market, where there was no lack of competition and reputations were free to rise or fall. The manufacturer might be identified by the mark which it was customary for him to put on every piece he sold or had woven. Cloth marks were made obligatory by a statute of 1536.[50] They were a valuable species of property, sometimes sold or bequeathed. In the sixteenth century, broadcloths or kerseys carrying the mark of Thomas Spring of Lavenham or John Winchcombe of Newbury commanded a premium on the foreign market;[51] half-a-dozen generations later pieces identified as the handiwork of a particularly skilful clothmaker were carefully noted at Aleppo by the factors of the City firm of Radcliffe, so that more might be ordered. But the chain of ownership was too lengthy to enable slipshod or deceitful workmanship easily to be brought home to the manufacturer. The instant way to ensure honest workmanship was by inspection when the cloth changed hands. This involved not merely unrolling the cumbersome pack to look for holes or other blemishes but also plunging the cloth into water to discover whether it shrank because it was over-stretched. This process of cloth-searching when applied to a broadcloth or even kersey of the old drapery took too much time and labour to be welcome to the vendor even when his wares passed the test, and was liable to generate ill-feeling. But there was no fool-proof alternative.

Attempts to standardise cloth sizes go back into the middle ages; and in the thirteenth century there had been legislation that authorised the inspection of cloths, at the place of manufacture, mostly in connection with the levy of the tax known as aulnage.[52] But the system in practice was not effective. Nor did the searchers appointed in the sixteenth century by the county justices bring much improvement, save perhaps in the west country. It was the merchants of the City who provided the driving force for the searching of cloths. They had been behind the succession of statutes that from time to time laid down the weights and dimensions of woollen cloths. These culminated in 1552 with the elaborate codifying act that has already been discussed.[53] Not long afterwards it evidently became clear at London that this statute could not be enforced merely by action at the places of manufacture, and that there must be intervention at the bottle-neck provided by the market at Blackwell Hall. Most City aldermen at this time were shippers of cloths; the Lord Treasurer was induced by the payment of a slightly higher rent to issue a lease of the aulnagership of London to the corporation; and in 1560 the country clothiers arriving with their manufactures were taken aback to find that a new and efficient team of cloth-searchers had been installed at Blackwell Hall itself.[54] Many were fined and no doubt mended their ways. The operation was ultimately challenged on legal grounds and seems to have lost momentum before the end of the century; certainly in 1601 the Privy Council was prodding the City into more lively action.[55] A generation or so later, the government of Charles I at the prompting of the merchants tried to tackle the problem at the seat of manufacture, and in 1630 dispatched to the west country industrial districts some commissioners armed with far-reaching powers of investigation. Their experiences proved dramatic and unpleasant, one of them being flung into the Wiltshire Avon for his pains. How much they managed to enliven the inspection of cloths is doubtful.

The troubled history of cloth-searching in England leaves the impression that the foreign buyer of English cloths had some genuine grievances, though John Leake, one of the searchers appointed by the City in 1560, acquitted the makers of fine west country broadcloths of over-stretching. Cloths were usually searched abroad as well as at home. In the days of the Antwerp mart, when the white undressed cloths of the Merchants Adventurers were normally dyed and finished by the Scheldt at the place of sale, there was an agreed procedure for settling the 'tare' or allowance for any shortcoming that was revealed when the bargain had been concluded, the pack opened and the cloths unfolded. Trouble really arose with the abandonment of the Antwerp mart, and when after 1582 the Merchants Adventurers were trying to establish their new headquarters at Middelburg on the island of Walcheren. There was said to be a scarcity of fresh water available for wetting the cloths. Besides, the purchasers were mostly agents acting for the real buyers who lived far to the north on the mainland in Holland, to whom the goods were at once forwarded. Defects were allegedly disclosed on opening the packs at their distant destinations. The English merchants came to suspect the fairness of this remote inspection, and tried to insist that cloth-searching should be at the place of sale, under the eye of vendor as well as purchaser. The Merchants Adventurers actually at one moment tried to enforce a rule that this should be a stipulation of sale written into each bargain.[56] English protests provoked resentment among the Hollanders, which was exacerbated by the political differences of the early seventeenth century, as well as by the rivalry of the textile interests of England and the United Provinces. In fact, the issue of the 'tare' provided an irritant that helped to sour Anglo-Dutch relations and to hasten the decline of the fortunes of the Merchants Adventurers in the Netherlands. There was no similar problem at Hamburg or other marketing centres where cloths were checked at the place of sale.

III   Clothmaking in English history: some social, fiscal and political impacts

7   The social framework

AS already remarked, the English woollen industry was a by-product of the human struggle for existence in a climate often indifferent and sometimes downright unfriendly. Those who consumed its output would hardly have been able to exist without it. But it deserves to be considered from the point of view of its producers as well as its consumers. From their standpoint, the industry justified itself on a different ground by providing or helping to provide a living for many thousands of men, women and even children in every generation during the quarter-millennium covered by this survey. These were the people, mostly humble and forgotten, who followed one or another of the various crafts whose application fructified in the completion of a piece of woollen cloth to serve the need for garments to be worn by all sorts and conditions in England, and beyond this, to meet the demand from nearby continental lands for quality textiles suited for wearing by the better-off. To an unknown extent, many of them were also engaged in agricultural labour. So far, this survey has been concerned mainly with the production and marketing of cloths; it is now time to look more closely at the people involved in these operations, who in themselves by their careers and achievements constituted a phenomenon of no small social and even political importance.

The craftsman who took a hand in one of the various occupations incidental to the processes of cloth manufacture did so in order to live, or live better, by the earning of money. Since these occupations, perhaps especially before the advance of the new draperies in the seventeenth century and particularly outside the towns, were mostly part-time, it is impracticable to offer a clear estimate of the numbers of persons involved in the industry, from the shearing of sheep to the packing of cloths. Possibly one person in ten of the whole population during the eighteenth century was in one way or another connected with the woollen industry.[57] In the sixteenth and early seventeenth century, woollen industries, mainly the preparatory processes before weaving, may have occupied 'the spare hours of at least one quarter of the cottage-farming population in England as a whole, and nearly half of that in the Midlands'.[58] We know that a score or more of people might successively share in the making of a broadcloth, but we cannot be sure how long it took them to complete it, either under conditions of maximum pressure or under the usual seasonal circumstances. Not much is known about real earnings either. Wage rates were fixed from 1563 onwards by the county justices for all crafts, largely on a piece-work basis. But even when statutory wage assessments were made and published, it was not always practicable to uphold them in the face of a collapsing market, the best-known instance being provided by the industrial crisis that convulsed the west country clothmakers in the early 1620s, during the opening phase of the Thirty Years' War in Germany.[59] On such occasions there was revealed the chequered element in the social benefits conferred by the textile industry upon its participants. Such infliction of hardship upon the work force has to be weighed against the enormous contribution of the cloth industry to the gross national output. We may at least be sure that in the absence of clothmaking for the market, everyone without exception would have lived more poorly.

The immediate benefit to most participants may seem modest, even in times of prosperity. But there were always exceptional individuals with an ability sufficient to use the industry as a personal ladder to well-being and affluence. From the earliest times, the woollen industry was generating its own wholesalers, entrepreneurs and employers in the clothmen or clothiers whose business it was to sell the cloths for further distribution rather than immediate consumption. They were the essential organisers whose activities linked manual workers and merchants. Though their social origins were usually modest and sometimes very humble, some of them rose to wealth and influence; a handful, like Jack of Newbury in the sixteenth century, won national fame, particularly in the buoyant years when the capacity of Antwerp mart seemed boundless. But ordinary business capacity imposed a limit to the ploughing-back of profits and the enlargement of stock-in-trade, so that successful clothiers often came to invest their accumulated funds in land. This was a process sufficiently widespread to excite the jealousy of neighbouring gentry, who in 1576 actually sought to invoke the authority of Parliament to hinder the acquisition of more than twenty acres by any clothier in the industrial region of the west country.[60] This did not prevent many clothiers from aping the gentry and even being welcomed into their ranks. Social mobility was vastly stimulated by industrial vigour, and the evidence of textile wealth is still visible all over the districts where the woollen industry once flourished. The 'great rebuilding' of English dwellings in stone that marked the sixteenth and seventeenth centuries owed much to a thriving woollen industry – witness the buildings put up at the expense of clothiers, from the fine town mansions of eighteenth-century Trowbridge in Wiltshire to the neat stone cottages at the bottom of the High Street in Burford, Oxfordshire, where an inscription on the front wall records that they were rebuilt in 1576 by the clothier Simon Wisdom, alderman of the town and founder of the school there, 'and given, with other tenements, to the same school'.

8   London, seat of the national cloth market

WHILE the progress of the woollen industry in the sixteenth century was marked by the development of an industrial population, particularly in the regions producing textiles for export, the most striking social growth occurred at London, the wholesale cloth distribution centre. London was at this time not notable for its manufactures, though it did produce some leather and metal wares. Its ancient Company of Weavers had sunk far into decline. But it was the chief market for the domestic cloth trade. Even more important, English cloth exports for most of the century were canalised along the short sea route from Thames to Scheldt. They were thus concentrated together for their passage to the foreign market at Antwerp for which London was the most convenient point of shipment. There was a corresponding import traffic in goods from the Netherlands. The population of the City had probably not risen to more than 50,000 during the fifteenth century; and although there was a persistent if spasmodic increase in the sixteenth, owing almost entirely to massive migration from the provinces, not until the 1570s did it pass the six-figure mark. From this source of labour there was supplied the manpower needed at the periodic freighting of the cloth-fleet for moving the tens of thousands of broadcloths and kerseys: for unpacking, brushing, folding and repacking them; for transferring them from Blackwell Hall to the merchants' warehouses; and finally at the quayside for putting them aboard the lighters that were usually employed to ferry them to the sea-going ships awaiting a downstream wind on the river. Craftsmen were sometimes needed to full and shear the semi-manufactured cloths arriving from the country, though before the seventeenth century dyeing and other finishing processes were mostly left to the purchaser abroad if the cloths were for

51

export.

The porters who conveyed the woollen cloths to the quayside also had to carry in the opposite direction the commodities comprising the import traffic encouraged by the export of English wares. Foremost among these were the linens and fustians, mostly originating in Germany or the Netherlands, that came in large quantity. These foreign products were no doubt much lighter to carry, but they often had to be 'finished', i.e. fulled, shorn and perhaps dyed, at London, before being distributed by drapers to the provinces. Fulling and shearing, whether of linens or woollens, were the business of the freemen of the City Companies of Fullers and Shearmen. From 1528 they were united as the Clothworkers' Company. This was a large and growing guild, sometimes aggressive in attitude, which soon elbowed its way to the forefront as one of the twelve major livery companies of London. One of its corporate grievances from the start was that there were numerous practising clothworkers in the City who belonged not to it but to other Companies, particularly the Merchant Taylors'. In fact, it never succeeded in embodying all clothworkers in its organisation. The control of labour in the cloth transit traffic at London was therefore always incomplete; porters and packers as well as fullers and shearmen competed for meagre wages in an ill-regulated market. This did not deter country lads from trudging to town in their hundreds to try their luck: at mid-sixteenth century over a fifth of all apprentices bound to the service of members of the 67 City companies belonged either to the Merchant Taylors' or Clothworkers'.[61] Some were destined to remain unskilled labourers while a few rose to wealth and honour. But they had all come because of the lure of a city expanding in wealth as well as in numbers. It is not unreasonable to infer that the extraordinary development of the Tudor City owed more to the flourishing transit traffic in textiles than to occasional meetings of Parliament or to the visits of rural litigants to the lawcourts at Westminster.

There also lived in the City, in addition to the porters and cloth-finishers, the merchants who had bought the woollen cloths from the country clothiers at Blackwell Hall. In the mid-sixteenth century, there were perhaps up to 300 of them, mostly men of modest origins, immigrants from the country, the sons of yeomen or husbandmen. Mercantile dynasties spanning more than a couple of generations were rare in the City. But to these men, the flowering of the cloth traffic in the sixteenth century brought wealth and power to a degree utterly without precedent in England. The annual value of the textiles passing through the hands of the exporting merchants at London *c*. 1560 was estimated by contemporaries to be approaching a million pounds sterling, to which should be added the cloths bought by drapers for distribution to the home market.[62] These may have been comparable in quantity but were probably for the most part coarser in quality so that their value need not be guessed as much more than half a million pounds. But these are gigantic sums when considered against the background of City and even national finance of the age.[63] English cloth shippers at this time almost all belonged to the Company of Merchants Adventurers – not a City but a national body, though in fact its outport membership was not very significant. London merchants by reason both of their numbers and their wealth dominated the Company, and although the Company headquarters lay in the Netherlands its London membership sometimes held informal meetings in the City, at Mercers' Hall or elsewhere, to resolve its mind about important issues of policy. By the second quarter of the sixteenth century the Court of Aldermen in the City was dominated by wealthy men from the Merchants Adventurers, from whose number most occupants of the mayoral seat for two or three generations continued to be drawn.

The rise of the cloth-export business was to exert a profound effect upon the guilds and companies of the City whose freedom, it may be recalled, was open only to their members. City freemen were by convention distinguished into two categories – the merchants, whose function was to buy and sell; and the artificers, who worked with their hands. The aldermen and other wealthy citizens fell into the first category, in particular those engaging in the import of potentially profitable wares such as wines, silks, spices and other oriental luxuries. The export of English products provided a means of paying for these in the foreign market. Thus down to 1527, the Company of Merchants Adventurers had a special administrative connection with the Mercers' Company; but even before then, many of its London members belonged to the Drapers', Grocers', Haberdashers' and other companies. At some unidentified moment in the sixteenth century, perhaps even earlier, it began to dawn upon Londoners that there was an adequate profit to be realised merely in the shipment of English woollen cloths, such was the demand for them, whether or not foreign wares were imported by the individual merchant in return. Certainly by the middle of the century many a merchant adventurer was content simply to dispose of his cloths at Antwerp for a bill of exchange payable at London, without having to bother himself about the finicky and risky business of acquiring some luxuries to ship home. As the years passed, less and less distinction remained to be drawn between the merchants of different livery companies whose livelihood was gained in the same woollen cloth traffic, whatever the City fraternity of their membership. This might seem a matter of small moment; but it fundamentally altered the nature of the livery companies of the City, which for some generations were to be ruled by a succession of flourishing cloth merchants, some also with an interest in the import of the foreign wares sometimes indicated by the title of the company, an increasing number of others without such an interest.

The halcyon age of the Merchants Adventurers in the City began to draw to a close in the last quarter of the sixteenth century with the disruption of the Antwerp mart followed by the feud with the Hanseatic League. Then in 1614 their charter was suspended, and although most of their privileges were restored in 1617 the good old times never quite returned. Meanwhile with the outbreak of war with Spain there were erstwhile cloth exporters who diverted their stock-in-trade to finance the dispatch of privateering expeditions; others found the retail trade of the City sufficiently remunerative. Under the first two Stuart kings there were new openings for City business men who were willing to farm the customs, pay for privileges of one sort or another, or simply lend money. Those still shipping woollen cloths had to join in the quest for new points of entry to the continental market. Others ventured further afield; but the extension of the pattern of English foreign trade was not necessarily to the benefit of the woollen cloth industry, whose products were scarcely marketable in the tropics. Thus the development of a direct traffic to the Baltic and the Levant in the late sixteenth century may well have helped the clothmakers, but the foundation of the East India Company in 1601 did not, since the Company found difficulty in disposing of any significant quantity of woollens. A new commercial age opened in the later seventeenth century, when Londoners diverted much of their trading capital to the reshipment of tropical products to consumers in central Europe. The woollen cloth trade, though still important, ceased to dominate the City, and the attachment of London to the woollen industry grew less exclusive. In any case, the ancient City institutions were losing their authority: in the eighteenth century Blackwell Hall factors, like other merchants, were not always concerned to take up their freedom of the City and the Halls of the livery companies were relinquished to retailers and artisans.

The long-lived and close attachment of the woollen industry to its London market left an indelible imprint upon commercial habits. This was not only owing to the enormous volume of the commodity traffic brought by the clothiers but, hardly less important, because it linked London intimately to Antwerp, the metropolis of world commerce. Antwerp as a business centre was an Italian outpost on the northern European coast, where southerners were the pace-setters in financial technique and business dealings. The granting of credit, often in the form of deferred payment for goods, had been commonplace in medieval London where the merchants had evolved ways and means of transferring debts, usually in satisfaction of other debts. The Italian mercantile colonies in the City had for centuries been transmitting some knowledge of their increasingly sophisticated business methods to the suspicious and sometimes resentful natives.[64] But only an inconspicuous corner of the national economy had been affected. Now in the sixteenth century the conduct of the cloth trade every year brought hundreds of young London merchants into the heart of an Italianate market, and the scale of controversial practices was vastly enhanced. Incidents and eccentricities hitherto little noticed because they were so unusual, were multiplied into visible abuses that seemed to cry out for a legal curb.

Hence the imprint of the cloth traffic to Antwerp may in good part be measured by the commercial legislation which the English government was impelled to frame. The giving and taking of interest, a misdemeanour hitherto cognisable in ecclesiastical courts, was regulated by statutes in 1487, 1545, 1552 and 1571 and so brought within the secular law;[65] the abuses of the Blackwell Hall market, as has been mentioned, were taken in hand in 1523;[66] and laws to deal with the controversial phenomenon of bankruptcy were enacted in 1543 and 1571.[67] Italian influence was also to be discerned in more private directions, notably in the publication of the earliest manual of book-keeping at London in 1543. Londoners were encouraged to use arabic rather than roman numerals; they began to keep accounts by double-entry, with all that this might imply for the analysis of turnover; and they were made more familiar with the mechanism of the international exchange system. Their co-operative partnerships grew in size and number, and merchants began to grasp the foreign concept of the 'firm' as something distinct from its individual participants. The vocabulary of the English language bears witness to the infiltration of Italian business terms at this time, from the 'posting' of entries in a ledger to the catastrophe of a 'bankruptcy'.[68] Such words and notions travelled to the City primarily through Antwerp, where they might be picked up by a visitor so poorly educated as the merchant adventurer John Isham, and thence carried home by the traders who regularly made their way to the cloth mart abroad to sell their broadcloths and kerseys.

The tycoons of the international cloth market powerfully affected the society from which they had sprung in yet other directions. There had been well-to-do merchants in the City in previous centuries; but never had capital been accumulated by so many and on such a scale. Some London merchants applied their methods to agriculture: there were many like John Isham, whose profits earned in the textile trade were sunk in the improvement of his estate in the country where he bought the manor of Lamport in Northamptonshire, or his contemporary

Thomas Revett, another cloth merchant but also a property owner and agricultural improver in Cambridgeshire. Examples might be multiplied, though the records do not permit the measurement of such investments. It was also to capital accumulated in the cloth trade that the development of mining and metallurgy after *c.* 1550 was largely due. Thus as early as the 1560s much of the capital for floating the Company of Mines Royal was subscribed by merchants adventurers, who also helped to supply the driving force for it and its sister venture the Company of Mineral and Battery Works. A London cloth-dealer (not the same man) was the initial Governor of each. A little later, London merchants are known to have been active in financing coal mines. Throughout the period, especially from *c.* 1540 onwards, the profits of the cloth traffic were often applied to found charitable institutions such as hospitals, almshouses and schools: the remarkable advance in literacy achieved by the English people by the middle of the seventeenth century may be identified as one fruit of this. Since the post-Reformation church was ill-suited to administer these charities, and there was no such organisation in England as the Portuguese *Misericordia*, benefactors seeking trustees for the maintenance of a charitable foundation tended to turn to the City company with which they were familiar.[69] This is why the livery companies swamped by merchants adventurers in the sixteenth century were in the eighteenth being transformed into charitable institutions whose main function nowadays remains the administration of endowments often dating from the prosperity of the Merchants Adventurers and the cloth trade.[70]

9   Taxes and politics

AT all times the fortunes of the woollen industry were related
to the favour of the English Crown. Its foreign policy might
help or hinder the merchants in their quest for access to foreign
markets, while on its domestic authority there hinged the law
and order essential to the smooth production of cloth. In
return, the Crown exacted its taxes. Their history is traceable
far back into the middle ages, though for present purposes it is
not necessary to look beyond the mid-fourteenth century, when
there crystallised out the fiscal arrangements that in their basic
form endured for two hundred years and were finally
abrogated only in the late seventeenth century. These
arrangements included the aulnage, an ancient levy invented
perhaps in the reign of Edward I. In the sixteenth century it
worked out at fourpence per statutory broadcloth, a figure that
by the early seventeenth century had crept up to sixpence, plus
a fee of a halfpenny for the local deputy aulnager who collected
the money. It had originally been part of his task to measure
each cloth to establish its conformity to the statutory
dimensions, after which he put his seal upon it; but long before
the sixteenth century this supervisory function seems generally
to have fallen into disuse.[71] The collection of aulnage in each
county was farmed out annually to the highest bidder, who
then took what he could in exchange for his seals from the
clothiers, without bothering much, if at all, about the
measurement of the cloths. Aulnage was a minor and probably
very inefficient tax, reckoned in the mid-sixteenth century to
yield an annual return of a few hundred pounds to the
exchequer. The office of aulnager for the whole kingdom was
granted by James I to his cousin the Duke of Lennox in April
1614, and thenceforth remained in the Lennox family.[72] The
duke doubtless sold the right to collect the tax in each county

for what he could get. Following parliamentary intervention in 1699, the tax lapsed in 1724.

Far more important than the aulnage were the customs duties, whose history can be carried back to the earliest administrative records. In the fourteenth century, Edward III made a renewed attempt to tap the wool and woollen cloth trades as sources of finance, and he promoted the organisation of the Company of Merchants of the Staple to facilitate the collection of export taxes and loans from the wool merchants. The fiscal system as he established it involved the heavy taxation of wool shipped abroad. It attracted a levy that by the later fifteenth century had settled down at £2 per sack, as payable by an English merchant.[73] The tax on cloths, likewise payable by the English exporter, was from 1347 fixed at the rate of fourteen pence on what in a later age was known as an undyed 'short cloth', i.e. the bulk of the textiles shipped to Antwerp in the sixteenth century.[74] One result of these fiscal arrangements was to supply the English textile manufacturer with a hidden protection against his continental rival using English wool to make cloth, since he had to pay much less tax on his products when shipped from English ports. No doubt this helps to explain the expansion of the continental market for cloths made in England in the fifteenth and sixteenth centuries. A further result that at the same time became painfully evident was the proportionate diminution of the customs receipts of the royal exchequer, as the shipments of the well-taxed wool were replaced by shipments of much more lightly-taxed cloths. The prosperity of the cloth industry under the early Tudors in this way paradoxically led to a marked fall in the king's revenue from customs receipts, and so helped to propel Henry VII and Henry VIII into the drastic courses that they sometimes followed in their quest for money.

The situation was partly retrieved in 1558, when the political tension that prevailed after the loss of Calais was exploited by the Lord Treasurer to revise customs rates. An important achievement now was a sharp increase in the duty on each 'short cloth' exported by Englishmen from 14d to 6s. 8d, the protests of the London merchants being subsequently met by an unofficial concession that in every pack of ten statutory 'short cloths' one should pass duty-free as a 'wrapper'. In effect, therefore, a duty of £3 was to be charged on each pack. Since so little raw wool was now being exported, it was a matter of less moment that the wool tax was also raised to £3 per sack, an equivalent in weight to approximately: four 'short cloths' or a little more. However, in the next reign the remaining disparity between the levies on cloth and wool was used in 1618 as an excuse by an even more hard-pressed monarch to increase further the cloth export tax by the levy of 'praetermitted customs', i.e. the sum allegedly necessary to balance the incidence of the cloth and wool rates. This was stated in 1621 to work out at a further 4s. 1d per west country broadcloth, and together with the extra levy needed to meet the demands of the Crown upon the Company of Merchants Adventurers, and also the discriminatory charges imposed by the States General of the United Provinces and the government of the Spanish Netherlands, left English textiles at a severe disadvantage in competing with native continental manufactures.[75] However, the epoch of high taxation proved to be short. The praetermitted customs were abolished by the Long Parliament in 1640.[76] Then at the Restoration in 1660 the cloth duty of 1558 on old draperies was halved.[77] Finally in 1699 all export taxes on cloths were abolished.[78] Other means of sustaining the apparatus of government had been found.

Direct financial interest was far from being the only motive that led the Crown to concern itself with the woollen industry. The great rulers of the sixteenth century, Henry VII, Henry VIII and Elizabeth I, were often in debt to the chief merchants of the City, with whom their ministers were sometimes on very close terms. This helps to explain how so much legislation dealing with the textile industry reached the statute book. Thus after the market setback at Antwerp in 1550 the conviction that standards of clothmaking were in need of improvement seems to have gained ground. So the law against middlemen in the wool trade was sharply fortified in 1552; and by a stringent Act of 1555 weavers in rural areas were forbidden to keep more than one loom and two apprentices and otherwise restricted in their occupation.[79] These enactments were in their way forerunners of the Statute of Apprentices of 1563, whose scope extended far beyond cloth manufacture.[80] Also connected with these enactments were the laws regulating the sizes of cloths, whose origins go back to the twelfth century if not earlier. These had been revised on many occasions since, and in 1552 were elaborated and brought up to date in the complex codifying statute which has already been mentioned.[81] This Act was itself subsequently revised more than once, the last occasion being in 1607,[82] after which the spread of the new draperies in all their variety, coupled with a certain lull in the output of new laws, made standardisation no longer practicable. In any case, the enforcement of the many laws purporting to regulate cloth manufacture was probably never more than patchy, especially outside the jurisdiction of the chartered boroughs. It was the shortcomings of aulnagers and other local officials in clothmaking regions that led the City of London in desperation to impose its own system of cloth-searching upon the country clothiers bringing wares to Blackwell Hall from 1560 onwards, as we have seen.[83]

On one persistent issue the English government and most of the City merchants were divided. The cloths shipped in such prodigious quantities by the Merchants Adventurers to Antwerp and their succeeding mart towns were for the most part white and unfinished. It was alleged that customers who bought them overseas liked to select their own colours for dyeing; besides, it was also said that the dyeing and other finishing processes were more skilfully done abroad than in England. On the other hand, there was the influential view that if it was preferable to export wool in the form of cloth rather than in the raw state then it was likewise better to ship cloth fully dressed and dyed than in a semi-manufactured state, 'unbarbed and unshorn'. This conviction lay behind parliamentary statutes of 1489, 1512, 1515 and 1536 by which the export of unfinished cloths was forbidden, save for coarse pieces below a certain market value.[84] The merchants were unable to prevent the passage of this prohibition, though they succeeded at each re-enactment in having the statutory value of a coarse cloth raised. In practice, their traffic was not blocked, since the Crown was happy to sell licences to flout the regulation. With the rise in the price-level at mid-century, the

61

prohibition became more sweeping than ever, but Elizabeth I was not willing to accept any more amending legislation. It was believed in the City that she preferred that the merchants should continue to buy the licences to continue their traffic.[85] In 1563, she granted the Merchants Adventurers a basic licence of unlimited duration for the shipment of 30,000 cloths each year. For the remainder of their shipments, they were expected to buy the other licences which the Queen issued to those whom she wished to oblige. It was for all parties a tolerable system: it did not visibly harm the cloth industry, it enabled the Queen to reward her servants at no personal cost to herself, and in return for their modest payments the merchants acquired legal security in their traffic.

But those who hoped to profit from the export of fully manufactured cloths were frustrated. The cloth-finishers of London, mostly though not all belonging to the Clothworkers' Company, were exasperated by the carriage of vast quantities of unfinished cloths under their eyes to the ships on the Thames, bound for the Netherlands. At an unguarded moment in the parliamentary session of 1566 the champions of the mercantile interest failed to stop the passage of a short Act by which one cloth in each pack of ten was thenceforth to be dyed and dressed before shipment, any licence to the contrary notwithstanding.[86] It was not vetoed by the Queen, and to a country gentleman sitting in the House might appear reasonable enough. But to a merchant adventurer it meant much expense of time and money in unwrapping the heavy packs delivered by the clothier, then taking out a cloth for dyeing, barbing and shearing, all in the knowledge that at the mart abroad the foreign buyer would pay less for the finished piece than for the unfinished. The little enactment was never fully nor for long enforced; but it aroused much passion and was a topic of acrimony for over a generation. Finally after the trade depression of the late 1590s the Queen in 1601 issued yet another licence, this time to the Earl of Cumberland, overriding the statute of 1566. However, the defeat of the clothworkers of London did not long endure. In 1614, on the advice of the London alderman Sir William Cockayne, James I called in the charter of the Merchants Adventurers, and all the licences, and turned the trade to north-west Europe, i.e. the market for most exports, over to an entirely new company whose purpose was to substitute the shipment of cloths dyed and dressed in place of the traditional semi-manufactured pieces. The motives of the King were complex and need not detain us.[87] What is clear is that he was unaware that he was playing into the hands of important Netherlands interests hostile or indifferent to the import of any English cloths at all. Within three years the impracticable nature of the project was manifest. The Merchants Adventurers had to be recalled and the licences reissued.

This painful experiment had far-reaching effects upon the cloth industry and trade. Distress and dislocation were caused in industrial districts, while in the City the traditional trust and respect of an important section of the mercantile community for the Crown was shaken. The Merchants Adventurers were not restored to all their old privileges. For renewing the liberty to export cloths undyed and undressed the Crown ultimately struck a hard bargain, the gist of which was that in return for the termination of Cumberland's licence (which involved regular payments to the Earl) the Company should pay £20,000 each year to the King. Thanks to the intervention of Cranfield, this was subsequently commuted for a capital sum.[88] The money for Company payments could only be found by collecting a levy from the merchants as they shipped their goods, and this new imposition no doubt helped further to discourage the ancient traffic in white semi-manufactured cloths, which never climbed back to its former volume. However, there can be no reasonable doubt that the sudden interruption of the trade in old draperies during the years 1614–17 lent a fillip to the manufacture of 'mingled coloured cloths, kerseys, bays, says, perpetuanas and divers other kinds of stuffs called the new draperies' in the country.[89] It was alleged on behalf of the Levant Company that there was an increased market for the finished cloths in the Mediterranean, where the Venetians were proving ineffective rivals, to offset in some measure the shrinkage of exports to the Netherlands.[90] Unfortunately for the merchants, after the lapse of Cumberland's grant the King did not cease to meddle. In 1623 he issued another similar licence to his Lennox cousin, whom he had already favoured by the lease of the aulnagership, so that this royal parasite could now draw sustenance from the woollen industry along two distinct channels.

It is scarcely surprising to find that by now the cloth shippers of the City had learnt to temper their relations with the Crown with a certain amount of coolness and even cynicism, nor that they played a prominent part in the quayside protest of 1629 when there was a brief concerted refusal by London merchants to pay the customs which Charles I in defiance of Parliament was exacting. But on the collapse of this demonstration, the Company of Merchants Adventurers swallowed its resentment and in a business-like way patched up its relations with the King. As to the Lennox export licence, the Company tried to make the best of a bad job and in 1632 came to an agreement with the Duchess of Richmond and Lennox to take out a lease, unhappily only to discover a few years later that the shipment of white undressed cloths had sunk so low that the rent could not be realistically financed. The Duchess stood on her rights.[91] But in a different field some progress seemed practicable. At the request of the Company, the government in 1631 agreed to dispatch commissioners to the west country, with the aim of remedying the defects in manufacture which hampered the sale of cloths abroad. But here too there arose snags. As we have seen, the royal agents met with obstruction and even violence in the manufacturing districts when they enquired into the arrangements for cloth-searching, so that it is difficult to be sure that their visits, which extended over several years, earned much other than ill-will.[92] The textile industry fared little better at the hands of the republican government twenty years later. When in 1654 Oliver Cromwell had the Dutch at his mercy, he refused to exploit the situation to make them reopen their market to English cloths. The plea of Edward Misselden, veteran agent of the Merchants Adventurers, he ignored.[93] Even more inconsiderately he picked a quarrel with the King of Spain, whose dominions supplied essential raw materials to the cloth industry and absorbed a quantity of its output.

In the later seventeenth century the status of the woollen industry underwent some change, as did the political world to which it had to accommodate itself. While the output of cloths was not in decline as a whole, the woollen manufacture no longer provided the only major source of employment in the kingdom beyond agriculture. The government depended for its revenue less upon the industry than had been the case before 1640. In the City too, the commodity trade had long ceased to be the only highroad to riches, and those who still followed it had lost their direct contacts with country manufacturers. They were often more interested in the re-export of tropical products, a business little connected with the woollen industry. Monopoly companies were under threat; the Merchants Adventurers lost their ancient privileges for ever in 1689, and the trade to most markets for woollen cloth lay open to unfettered competition. Perhaps this helps to explain why the profits of merchants seem to have been running at a more modest level.[94] The last mercantile giant of the traditional sort that was typified in the careers of the three Gresham brothers in the reign of Henry VIII was probably Lionel Cranfield, merchant adventurer and free of the Mercers' Company, who began his operations in the 1590s as a cloth exporter. It was a sign of the times that he soon deserted this for high finance, farming the customs and lending money to the Crown, and ultimately rose to be Lord Treasurer and Earl of Middlesex. Indeed, most of his wealth seems to have been accumulated after he had left the City for the Court.[95]

The woollen industry adapted its political defences after the Restoration to the changing structure of political power. In the new age of party politics the woollen interest found friends in Parliament and among the pamphleteers who were taking advantage of the nascent freedom of the press. Among these allies could be heard a voice of industry sufficiently loud to achieve not only the dismantling of the cloth export taxes but also the abolition of the privileges of the Merchants Adventurers (1689) 'for the better encouragement of the manufacture as well as the growth of wool'.[96] In 1697 the Commons refused to authorise a domestic tax on cloth.[97] A practical demonstration of encouragement was to be seen in the wearing of garments of English woollen cloth by Charles II himself; and in 1666 it was enacted by Parliament that 'for the

65

encouraging of the woollen manufactures of this Kingdom' deceased persons were to be buried 'in a shirt, shift or sheet of wool only'.[98] A striking demonstration of power was offered when, as a result of the emigration of clothmaking artificers to Munster from the west country, Irish serges began to compete with English in the Dutch market. At first this did not seem of consequence but it led to resentment during the wartime depression of the 1690s. There arose an outcry from west country clothiers, seeking the diversion of the Irish to the making of linen instead of woollen textiles. A bill to prohibit the export of wool and woollen cloths from Ireland to the continent was introduced at Westminster; it passed into law in 1699 not so much, however, because of any intrinsic merits as because of the support of the parliamentary opposition, which seized on it as a measure to humiliate and overthrow an already tottering ministry.[99] Some at least of the emigrants from the west country now returned home.

For some generations the East India Company, founded in 1601, provided a major target for the hostility of the woollen interest. At an early stage, it came under fire for exporting bullion instead of woollen cloths. When it was granted a new charter in 1693, one condition was that it should export every year English merchandise to the value of £100,000, i.e. in effect woollen textiles. Woollen cloths were in fact little consumed in India, where all too often they rotted away in warehouses. Such demand as there was in the Indian market was for old draperies, which were used for furnishing or military purposes. The Company was also inadvertently offering provocation from the 1670s onwards by increasing the import of oriental calicoes and silks. These were nervously denounced as stealing the domestic English market from native English manufacturers. No doubt there was a marginal field of competition, particularly in the lighter and more fanciful sorts of textile, whether for clothing or household purposes. Nevertheless, silks and cottons could only be considered substitutes for woollens to a very limited extent. However, East India wares figured prominently among the goods on which impositions were laid in 1690, calicoes attracting a new duty of 20 per cent, with a rebate on re-export.[100] Then a statute of

1699 clapped a further duty of 15 per cent on eastern silks, muslins and so forth, similarly with arrangements for a rebate on re-export.[101] As such measures were alleged to provide an inducement to copy the patterns of eastern designs and so facilitate smuggling, a subsequent Act in 1720 prohibited the use or wearing of any printed, painted, stained or dyed calico in any garment or apparel whatever; and it was forbidden to expose for sale any furniture containing such unless it were intended for export.[102] To mollify an alarmist sectional clamour, the arm of the law could hardly be further stretched.

10 *Some general reflections*

THE paradox of clothmaking in early modern England has now been laid bare. It provided an occupation for artificers of both sexes who practised their craft over wide areas of the countryside and, especially in the sixteenth and seventeenth centuries, were for the most part also tethered to the tasks of agriculture: yet at the same time their industry was not at all limited by the frontiers of an insular market but provided a major current in the international commodity traffic, large enough to furnish a prominent component of the world market at Antwerp. Domestically, it was now the chief engine by which the English economy was swept past its medieval station as a purveyor of raw materials for the neighbouring continent and taken to the very portals of the industrial revolution. The leading men in this movement, whether commercial or industrial, were enabled to accumulate capital surplus to their stock-in-trade needs and therefore available for investment in other fields. And so the woollen manufacture and trade in less than half-a-dozen generations made possible an accumulation of capital that was used with a multiplier effect for the transformation of agriculture, the renovation of dwelling-places of all sizes, the accelerated exploitation of domestic mineral resources, the provision of educational and other social charities all over the kingdom, and the rise of the City of London as a world-wide financial centre.[103] The woollen industry was also linked directly with the development of communications: not merely the repair of bridges and roads, purposes for which London merchants of the sixteenth century sometimes bequeathed money, but also the improvement of river navigation. Thus the streams of Aire and Calder were deepened at the beginning of the eighteenth century primarily for the benefit of the Yorkshire woollen industry.

The making and marketing of cloths at the same time also presented a genuine invitation to individual material betterment. It offered a social ladder to a minority of gifted and determined men who in a previous generation might well have lived out their lives as peasants or craftsmen. The families of such successful clothiers or merchants sometimes fell back into their original obscurity, leaving little or no mark in the records. But a significant number succeeded in entering the ranks of the country gentry: there is no lack of evidence to document stories of upward social mobility. Particularly in the years of prosperity in the sixteenth century, clothmaking on a scale hitherto unparalleled made practicable a mingling of fresh strains with the property-owning and governing families of the kingdom. With good reason, genealogists have identified the sixteenth century as the age during which these families were refreshed by the largest infusion of new blood since the Norman Conquest 500 years previously. The main highway of the newcomers led them through the City of London, particularly in the sixteenth century, though there were some by-ways following other routes. The City was enriched by their passage; its growing wealth may be measured, for instance, by the increased yield of its customs, or the unprecedented ability of its citizens to lend money to the English crown. Thus the foreign debt which Henry VIII incurred from *c.* 1545 onwards, which saddled him and his successors with heavy payments to the Fuggers and other continental banking houses, was ultimately paid off by his daughter thirty years later by calling on the rich men of the City, almost all cloth-dealers, for their help. Her agent in this achievement was the wholesale cloth merchant Thomas Gresham, whose activities marked the emergence of London as an independent and international financial centre.

From the point of view of the government, especially with the raising of the cloth export duty in 1558, the yield of taxes from the woollen industry was vital. For some decades, the annual shipment of cloths from the port of London rarely fell below the equivalent of 100,000 'short cloths', and sometimes rose well above this. Accordingly, in normal years the royal exchequer was able to collect a gross sum of £30,000 from the cloth dealers in the Company of Merchants Adventurers, a sum whose significance may be judged by the fact that Elizabeth Tudor seems to have regarded £40,000 as a suitable upper limit for the maintenance of her household, i.e. the chief spending department of her government. Customs receipts, mostly connected with the cloth trade in one way or another, continued to provide the major source of royal revenue, apart from the direct taxes for whose levy an express parliamentary consent was required. Although the wool tax, once the major source of money for the Crown, dwindled away in the sixteenth century and came to an end when the export of wool was terminated in 1614, the progress of the new draperies was opening up a new field with the large-scale shipments of coloured cloths: thus by the 1630s about a tenth of the customs receipts arising from goods imported by English merchants at London was derived from dyestuffs, chiefly cochineal and indigo.[104] It was an enhanced customs yield drawn chiefly from the cloth industry that made Elizabeth Tudor relatively independent of her parliaments and that enabled her two successors to maintain themselves in the abeyance of these awkward assemblies.

The cloth export tax, relatively light until 1558, could safely be increased because of the almost insatiable foreign demand. In 1509 the municipal rulers of Antwerp were content to accede to every wish of the Merchants Adventurers, if only the Englishmen would agree to fix their cloth mart beside the Scheldt. English cloths provided until 1569 an essential element of the turnover at the international market of Antwerp, where their annual value on the commodity Bourse was exceeded only by that of the silks imported from Italy; and they attracted purchasers from all over central Europe.[105] The imposition of the greatly enhanced tax from 1558 was a source of envy and irritation to the neighbours of Elizabeth I, from Philip of Spain to the King of Denmark, who were angrily aware that when their subjects bought fine English broadcloth, which continued to maintain its reputation in the retail market, they were putting so much money into the English exchequer. Nor did their successors in subsequent generations readily acquiesce in the situation; but neither the Dutch in the first half of the seventeenth century nor the French in the second were able to provide more than a partly successful rivalry to the ubiquitous English woollen cloths. To investigate the importance of the textile interest in English foreign policy does not lie within the framework of this survey. But it should not be forgotten that the maintenance and even the expansion of the continental market for English woollen cloths was an aim that underlay the dealings of Henry VII with the rulers of the Burgundian Netherlands as much as the conclusion of the Methuen Treaty with Portugal by the ministers of Queen Anne in 1703, or Walpole's commercial agreement with Russia in 1734.

The circumstances in which the English woollen industry was enabled to flourish within the commodity trade of western Europe during the centuries of the Tudor and Stuart monarchs were varied. Any enumeration would necessarily include the quality of the wool originally available in the Welsh Marches and the Cotswolds, and the traditional skills applied at the loom and the spinning-wheel. But none deserves to be rated more highly than the insular security of the kingdom, which made practicable a degree of public order hardly paralleled elsewhere in Europe. There was civil war in the 1640s and some moments of disturbance in the 1650s; the port of Bristol and the clothmaking town of Colchester suffered serious damage. But there was never any thoroughgoing devastation comparable to the burning and pillaging which in 1582 extinguished industrial activity for years at the previously flourishing Flemish textile centre of Hondschoote.[106] Both the Netherlands and northern Italy, where the major trade rivals of the English cloth manufacture were seated, were at one time or another in the sixteenth century important theatres of war and suffered severely. But even during the first English civil war, when London was firmly held for the Parliament while many clothmaking districts remained under the control of the king, the output of cloths was nowhere brought to a halt for long. During the actual hostilities, 1643–5, the hallage receipts at Blackwell Hall declined only moderately, and soon more than recovered.[107] Evidently the country clothiers were only to a small extent impeded in the delivery of their cloths to the national market.

Scores of parliamentary acts concerning the woollen industry reached the statute-book during the 250 years covered in this survey. They tell the historian a great deal about the stresses and controversies provoked by the making of cloths, but he is not entitled to use them as evidence of governmental control over the industry. At all times and stages, clothmaking was controlled by the market. Virtually alone, it made practicable the gradual supersession of old by new draperies, which is the central story of the industry: the intervention of the Crown when it forbade the export of unfinished cloths in 1614 at most slightly hastened the process. Statutes that offended a powerful interest, such as the Act of 1566 requiring the finishing of every tenth cloth, were fought if necessary for decades, while those that negated essential needs, such as the prohibition of the trade of middlemen in wool, were either ignored or soon repealed at least in part.[108] Outside the corporate boroughs, where enforcement of industrial legislation tended to be relatively close, obedience to the law was very patchy, so that, for instance, it is difficult to generalise about the application of the apprenticeship regulations. But when the requirements of the market were taken up by the merchants, a strong coercive power was generated. Thus the City was able to persuade successive parliaments to standardise the weights and dimensions of the old draperies. When the local authorities proved incapable of enforcing the new statute, the Londoners craftily bought the right to do so themselves and, so armed, pounced upon the country clothiers who had dared to present their faulty fabrics at Blackwell Hall.[109] But this sort of rough coercion was never effective for long; the long-term solution was ultimately provided by the more intimate connection of the factors of Blackwell Hall with the manufacturers of the new draperies, whose sizes were not laid down by Parliament, but left to conform to market demands in freedom.

Appendix

IS THE ANNUAL OUTPUT OF ENGLISH WOOLLEN CLOTHS MEASURABLE?

ENGLISHMEN before the very late seventeenth century were little concerned to gather statistics save very occasionally and for immediate practical purposes. Historians bent upon quantification must chiefly turn to such records of taxes and fees as survive. The one tax attracted by all cloths was the aulnage; but the right to collect it was farmed out early, and the extant aulnage records have been shown to be of little use for purposes of measurement, by E. M. Carus-Wilson, 'The Aulnage accounts: a criticism', *Economic History Review,* II (1929–30) 114–123.

It is however practicable to learn something about the portion of the cloth output that was shipped abroad, from the surviving customs records. For the sixteenth and early seventeenth centuries these are copious though far from complete. For the period 1642–60 they almost completely fail us, and are less satisfactory for the later than the earlier seventeenth century. Much information has been drawn from the customs returns and put into print, either directly or in summary form: the most important publications carrying them include the following. There are tables of wool and cloth exports in *England's Export Trade 1275–1547,* ed. E. M. Carus-Wilson and Olive Coleman (Oxford, 1963) and, for the mid-sixteenth century, in J. D. Gould, *The Great Debasement* (Oxford, 1970). Figures drawn from customs returns have also been printed by F. J. Fisher, 'Commercial trends and policy in sixteenth-century England', *Economic History Review,* X (1939–40) 95–117; A. Friis, *Alderman Cockayne's Project and the cloth trade* (Copenhagen and London, 1927); W. B. Stephens, 'The cloth exports of the provincial ports, 1600–1640', *Economic History Review,* 2nd ser., XXII (1969) 228–48; B. E. Supple, *Commercial Crisis and Change in England 1600–1642* (Cambridge, 1959). The office of Inspector-General of Imports and Exports was created in 1696, and figures gathered for him from the merchants' returns have been tabulated by E. B. Schumpeter, *English overseas trade statistics 1697–1808* (Oxford, 1960).

The interpretation of the figures collected from customs records is fraught with problems. The incidence of smuggling may well have lessened the customs totals for the earlier period, while for the later there remains a suspicion that the merchants tended to exaggerate the size of their shipments. The efficiency (if not the honesty) of customs officers varied from time to time and place to place. It must also be borne in mind that from 1559 the merchants at London were permitted to ship one cloth in every pack of ten as a 'wrapper' free of tax. A further favour was granted to the merchants of Hull, York and other northern ports, who from 1560 were allowed to count two cloths in ten as duty-free 'double-wrappers'. This 'double-wrapper' concession was extended in June 1591 to the merchants of Exeter and the south-west, probably though not certainly for the first time (*see* Queen to exchequer officers, 24 June 1591, SP 12/239/54). It is therefore essential before citing customs figures to consult the commentaries of historians, some of which are embodied in the works cited above. There is also G. N. Clark, *Guide to English Commercial Statistics 1696–1782* (London, 1938) and three indispensable papers by R. Davis in successive numbers of the *Economic History Review,* 2nd ser., 'English foreign trade, 1660–1700', VII (1954–5) 150–166; 'English foreign trade, 1700–1774', XV (1962–3) 285–303; 'The Rise of Protection in England', XIX (1966) 307–317; and Phyllis Deane, 'The output of the British woollen industry in the eighteenth century', *Journal of Economic History,* 17 (1957) 207–223.

The surest figures for shipments of woollen cloths relate to exports by the East India Company, since they originate from the private ledger books, journals and other records of the Company and not from customs documents. They have been sorted and tabulated by K. N. Chaudhuri, *The Trading World of Asia and the English East India Company 1660–1760* (Cambridge, 1978) 513–6. Unfortunately, they refer only to a small and unrepresentative fraction of total exports.

A serious obstacle, hitherto insurmountable, stands in the path of anyone trying to squeeze from the customs documents a continuous series of figures covering cloth shipments throughout the period under consideration. It springs from the fact that old draperies, which predominated in the sixteenth century, were taxed by the statutory piece irrespective of value, so that no higher tax was payable on a fine than on a coarse broadcloth or kersey. On the other hand, the new draperies were taxed or recorded (from 1699) according to their official or alleged market value. The problems involved in trying to equate numbers and values of textile shipments when these included quantities of draperies old and new were first exposed by

F. J. Fisher, 'London's export trade in the early seventeenth century', *EcHR,* 2nd ser., III (1950–1) 151–161, who concluded that they are ultimately insoluble. This is also much the view of W. B. Stephens, 'Further observations in English cloth exports, 1600–1640', *EcHR,* 2nd ser.,XXIV (1971) 253–7. To add to the complexities, the exchequer enrolment practice until very early in the seventeenth century was to segregate receipts from shipments of old draperies apart from those of general merchandise, including the early new draperies. This has misled some historians into the assumption that the exports of old draperies in the last quarter of the sixteenth century might, as previously, be equated with total exports of woollen cloths.

A vantage point on firmer ground has recently been discovered by D. W. Jones, who has tabulated and printed 'The "Hallage" Receipts of the London Cloth Markets, 1562–1720', *Economic History Review,* 2nd ser., XXV (1972) 567–87. His figures point to a long-term rising trend of textile traffic at Blackwell Hall, though he has indicated various reservations that must be made about them. They do not cover Norwich and Norfolk textiles, which were generally exempt from the marketing regulations, nor cloths changing hands locally or at fairs, and the interpretation of the accounts is complicated by the mingling of the lodging charges on cloths remaining unsold over the first week-end with the entry fee. But Dr Jones's hallage data do furnish valuable information about the rise of the new draperies and fluctuations of trade. His comments on the organisation of the central cloth market, as well as his tables of figures, have been used without further acknowledgement in the text above, but those seeking fuller information should consult Dr Jones's article.

From the finished or semi-finished product we turn in search of a yardstick to the raw material. Gregory King's estimate of a total sheep population of 12,000,000 for England and Wales in the late seventeenth century has not been rejected as a reasonable guess by at least one modern authority – R. Trow-Smith, *British Livestock Husbandry to 1700* (London, 1957) p. 233. It is unlikely that the number of sheep a century and half earlier was greater than this – indeed, it may have been less, perhaps much less. In mid-sixteenth century a venturesome observer put the sheep population that produced the wool and woollen cloths then being shipped each year at 8,400,000 odd – Tawney and Power, *Tudor Economic Documents,* see I, 180. Bearing these surmises in mind, it might be very tentatively suggested that at the earlier period something like two-thirds of the annual wool clip was finding its way abroad, either raw or in the form of textiles. This of course involves acceptance of a plausible though unverifiable premiss – that imports of wool from Ireland and elsewhere were being balanced by the exports of wool by Staplers and licencees. Another reservation must be made with regard to the stability of cloth exports, which at times of war or trade crisis naturally diminished though the wool clip remained constant. See p. 33–4 above. Conversely, when the harvest failed and food prices accordingly rose, it was the turn of the domestic market for textiles to contract.

Since historians are baffled by the problem of equating shipments of old and new draperies, it is not practicable to compile any continuous and inclusive index for the shipment of woollen cloths during the period under consideration. At most, it is possible to offer an intuitive surmise covering export quantities. We know from customs documents in the 1550s, despite the many gaps in their number, that during this decade, when output was still confined to old draperies, exports were running at a level at least 50 per cent higher than in the first decade of the sixteenth century. Further, at the end of the decade, *c.* 1560, there seems to have been a certain consensus of opinion in valuing the cloths shipped each year from London to Antwerp at rather less than £1,000,000; the merchant George Nedham put it at £920,000 (G. D. Ramsay, *The politics of a Tudor merchant adventurer* (Manchester, 1979) p.96). It is a fair estimate that London cloth shipments to Spain and other peripheral markets, together with the outport exports to all destinations, made the difference up to the round figure of £1,000,000. This rough calculation of £1,000,000 as the value of all cloth shipments at this moment is not in conflict with other evidence from documents of the period.

From the end of the seventeenth century, the customs valuations of all woollens shipped abroad each year have been printed by Mrs Schumpeter, *English overseas trade statistics*. The figures may be slightly exaggerated, but are substantially reliable. For the ten years 1731–40, a decade of comparative peace, woollen exports were running at an average annual valuation of £4,147,294, i.e. rather more than four times the £1,000,000 suggested for *c.* 1560. If the price of cloths had only remained stable over the intervening 170–180 years, it would follow that the exports of the woollen industry had more than quadrupled during this period. Unfortunately, no such assurance is available. Not only had the character of the textile output been transformed, but there are sundry hints that cloth prices were rising, though not as steeply as during the first sixty years of the sixteenth century. What we do know is that the cost of simple necessities of life had approximately doubled during the period 1560–1740, though other goods, such as glass, salt and tropical produce, had become more plentiful and cheaper. A sense of direction, admittedly impressionistic, may be derived from contemplation of the fairly persistently rising revenue collected at Blackwell Hall from the cloths arriving at London for sale, which conjures up the picture of a generally expanding industry: the annual hallage receipts at Blackwell Hall are shown by Dr Jones to have more than doubled in the course of the seventeenth century, despite a suspected (though unproven) development of direct contacts between manufacturer and retailer. Perhaps the nearest we can ever get to the truth is the very tentative estimate that in the period 1560–1740 English woollen textiles shipped to overseas markets had increased in value by a factor of two to three. Or more prudently, we might content ourselves with an even more imprecise but still important deduction: that whatever the short-term fluctuations of trade, and despite some serious crises, the foreign as well as the domestic market for English woollen cloths was on balance more, possibly much more, than sustained.

Notes and References

1. 11 Edw. III.

2. The clothmaking processes have often been described. See *A history of technology*, III, eds. C. Singer *et al.* (Oxford, 1957) 151–205; W. Endrei, *L'Evolution des techniques du filage et du tissage* (Paris, 1969). There are useful comments in K. G. Ponting, *The woollen industry of south-west England* (Bath 1971) and in his preface to *Baines's Account of the Woollen Manufacture of England* (Newton Abbot, 1970).

3. M. F. Mazzaoui, *The Italian cotton industry in the later middle ages* (Cambridge, 1981) 78, 82; M. Hoffman, *The warp-weighted loom* (Oslo, 1964) ch. iv; R. V. Lennard, 'An early fulling mill: a note', *Economic History Review (EcHR)* XVII (1947) 150.

4. 5 & 6 Edw. VI c. 6, sect. xii.

5. 1 Ric. III c. 8.

6. A. P. Wadsworth and J. de L. Mann. *The cotton trade and industrial Lancashire 1600–1780* (Manchester, 1931) 97–108, 411–31.

7. 5 & 6 Edw. VI c. 6.

8. Some misplaced erudition has been used to supply an oriental origin to the name – see *The Journal of European Economic History*, V (1976) 584.

9. 'Information of frauds', undated *c.* 1592, SP 12/243/114.

10. Evidence in the lawsuit of Hastings *v.* Clarke *et al.*, E 133/3/434.

11. Staplers to Hollanders, September 1578, pr. *Bronnen tot de geschiedenis van den handel met Engeland* & c., ed. H. J. Smit, I, ii ('s-Gravenhage, 1950) no. 1376.

12. Royal proclamation, 26 September 1614.

13. 5 & 6 Edw. VI c. 7.

14. G. D. Ramsay, 'The Merchants of the Staple and the down-fall of the English wool export traffic', *La lana come materia prima, Atti della Prima Settimana di Studio, Prato* (Florence, 1974) 53–6.

15. J. H. Munro, 'Wool-price schedules and the qualities of English wools in the later middle ages', *Textile History*, 9 (1978) 118–69.

16. 4 Hen. VII c. 11; 21 Hen. VII c. 1; 37 Hen. VIII c. 15; 5 & 6

Edw. VI c. 7.

17. 1 Edw. VI c. 6; 1 & 2 Ph. & M. c. 13; W. B. Crump and G. Ghorbal, *History of the Huddersfield woollen industry* (Huddersfield, 1935) 33.

18. The replies to the enquiry are at SP 12/114.

19. 'The defence of the Staplers', *c.* 1652, SP 18/25/42.

20. T. S. Willan, 'Manchester Clothiers in the early seventeenth century', *Textile History*, 10 (1979) 175–83.

21. 'Old and New Draperies compared' in J. Thirsk and J. P. Cooper (eds), *Seventeenth-Century Economic Documents* (Oxford, 1972), p.204.

22. M. J. Dickenson, 'Fulling in the West Riding woollen cloth industry 1689–1770', *Textile History* 10 (1979) 127–41.

23. J. de L. Mann, 'Clothiers and weavers in Wiltshire during the eighteenth century', in L. S. Pressnell (ed.), *Studies in the Industrial Revolution*, (London 1960) 93; S. and B. Webb, *The History of Trade Unionism*, new edn (London, 1920) 32–7; C. R. Dobson, *Masters and Journeymen: A Prehistory of Industrial Relations, 1717–1800* (London, 1980) *passim.*

24. Wage assessment problems have been discussed by D. Woodward, 'Wage rates and living standards in pre-industrial England', *Past and Present*, 91 (1981) 28–46.

25. Stated in the text of stat. 2 & 3 Ph. & M. c. 14.

26. List printed by W. G. Hoskins, *Local History in England* (London, 1959) 177.

27. R. B. Smith, *Land and Politics in the England of Henry VIII. The West Riding of Yorkshire: 1530–46* (Oxford, 1970) 115–18.

28. V. Skipp, *Crisis and Development. An ecological case study of the Forest of Arden 1570–1674* (Cambridge, 1978) 59. See also J. Thirsk, 'Industries in the Countryside', in F. J. Fisher (ed.), *Essays in the Economic and Social History of Tudor and Stuart England* (Cambridge, 1961) 70–88.

29. Noted by A. H. Johnson, *The history of the worshipful company of Drapers of London*, II (London, 1915) 169–71.

30. 14 & 15 Hen. VIII c. 1. See p. 41.

31. Blackwell Hall draft regulations, Michaelmas 1518, Guildhall, Journals, II, ff. 366v–67.

32. Certificate of Yorkshire justices, 28 January 1591, SP 46/18, ff. 273v–76.

33. Thirsk and Cooper (eds), *Seventeenth-Century Economic Documents*, 471.

34. P. Deane, 'The output of the British woollen industry' 221.

79

35. See appendix on the measurement of output.

36. H. Amman, 'Deutschland und die Tuchindustrie nordwest-Europas im Mittelalter', *Hansische Geschichtsblätter*, LXXII (1954) 1–63; for the general situation, E. M. Carus-Wilson, 'The Woollen Industry', *Cambridge Economic History of Europe*, II (1952) 355–428.

37. H. Amman, 'Die Friedberger Messen', *Rheinische Vierteljahrsblätter*, 15/16 (Bonn, 1951) 192–225.

38. Merchants Adventurers to Privy Council, 20 January 1564, SP 12/15/67. This document was printed by H. J. Smit, *Bronnen*, I, no. 985.

39. J. I. Israel, 'Spanish wool exports and the European economy, 1610–40', *EcHR*, 2nd ser., XXXIII (1980) 193–211.

40. See p. 33.

41. V. Kostić, *Ragusa and England 1300–1650* (Belgrade, 1975) 576–82.

42. T. S. Willan, *The Muscovy Merchants of 1555* (Manchester, 1953) 4.

43. J. Stow, in C. L. Kingsford (ed.), *Survey of London*, (Oxford, 1908) I, 189.

44. 14 & 15 Hen. VIII c. 1. See p. 33.

45. Blackwell Hall draft regulations, 1518, Guildhall, Journals, II, ff. 366–7.

46. For hallage, see p. 75.

47. See p. 33.

48. 'The complaints of the Drapers', c. May 1622, SP 14/130/141; G. Unwin, *Industrial Organization in the sixteenth and seventeenth centuries* (Oxford, 1904) 112–14.

49. 8 and 9 Will. III c. 9.

50. 27 Hen. VIII c. 12.

51. 'Certain things to be considered', undated c. 1569, SP 12/185/101.

52. For more information on aulnage see p. 58.

53. 5 & 6 Edw. VI c. 6; see also p. 13.

54. City report to Burghley, 23 April 1588, SP 46/35, f. 39.

55. *Acts of the Privy Council 1600–1*, 445–6, 473–4 &c.

56. The situation was clarified by Secretary Skinner of the Merchants Adventurers in his memorandum of 3 December 1629, SP 16/153/7. On the Dutch side, the authority is N. W. Posthumus, *De nationale organisatie der lakenkoopers tijdens de republiek* (Utrecht, 1927). See also C. H. Wilson, 'Cloth production and international competition in the seventeenth century', *EcHR*, 2nd ser. XIII (1960–1) 209–21.

57. Deane, 'The output of the British woollen industry', 213.

58. A. Everitt in J. Thirsk (ed.), *The Agrarian History of England and Wales*, IV (Cambridge, 1967) 425.

59. On the problem of wages, see pp. 27–8.

60. 18 Eliz. c. 6, sec. iii.

61. G. D. Ramsay, 'The recruitment and fortunes of some London freemen in the mid-sixteenth century', *EcHR*, 2nd ser. XXXI (1978) 532.

62. See the Appendix.

63. Ibid.

64. For medieval business practices see M. Postan, *Medieval trade and finance* (Cambridge, 1973) 1–91.

65. 3 Hen. VII c. 5; 37 Hen. VIII c. 9; 5 & 6 Edw. VI c. 20; 13 Eliz. c. 8.

66. 14 & 15 Hen. VIII c. 8; see p. 41.

67. 33 Hen. VIII c. 4; 13 Eliz. c. 7.

68. There is further evidence on this topic in F. Edler, *Glossary of medieval terms of business. Italian series 1200–1600* (Cambridge, Mass., 1934).

69. W. K. Jordan, *The Charities of London 1480–1660* (London, 1960) *passim*; for the Portuguese *Misericordia*, A. J. R. Russell-Wood, *Fidalgos and Philanthropists* (London, 1968).

70. See the *Report of the Parliamentary Commission on the City of London Livery Companies* (1884) 41 *et passim*.

71. For the early history of aulnage, A. Friis, *Alderman Cockayne's Project and the Cloth Trade* (Copenhagen and London 1927) 31–5.

72. The grant was entered on the Patent Roll for 13 & 14 April 1614, C 66/1978, mm. 10, 13.

73. N. S. B. Gras, *The Early English Customs System* (Cambridge, Mass., 1918) 602.

74. Ibid., 72. A complex situation has been summarised in my text. Foreign merchants paid at higher rates.

75. Thirsk and Cooper (eds), *Seventeenth-Century Economic Documents*, 475–6 *et passim*; detailed charges were listed in the parliamentary committee report at Chatsworth House, MS. H. 48, ff. 50–1.

76. 16 Car. I cc. 12 & 25.

77. 12 Car. II c. 4, Book of Rates appended.

78. 11 Will. III c. 20.

79. 5 and 6 Edw. VI c. 7; 2 and 3 Ph. & M. c. 11.

80. 5 Eliz. c. 4.

81. See p. 13.

82. 4 Jac. I c. 2.

83. See p. 46.

84. 3 Hen. VII c. 12; 3 Hen. VIII c. 7; 5 Hen. VIII c. 3; and 27 Hen. VIII c. 13.

85. Anon. memorandum on the cloth trade, March 1613, SP 14/72/70.

86. 8 Eliz. c. 6.

87. See the brief summary by R. Ashton, *The City and the Court 1603–1643* (Cambridge, 1979) 105–6.

88. Details in anon. to king, 26 March 1635, SP 16/285/46.

89. Interlopers' petition to Parliament, 1621, Chatsworth House MS. H. 48, f. 22v.

90. Report of the Levant Company to Parliament, 1621, ibid., 23v.

91. Merchants Adventurers to Council, 28 August 1636, SP 16/330/79; ibid. to Council for Trade, undated *c*. December 1661, Add. MS. 25, 115, ff. 327–46.

92. See p. 46.

93. Misselden to Protector, 8/18 December 1654, *Thurloe State Papers* (London, 1742) 13–14.

94. R. B. Grassby, 'The rate of profit in seventeenth-century England', *English Historical Review*, LXXXIV (1969) 721–51. cf. above, p. 25.

95. M. Prestwich, *Cranfield. Politics and Profits under the Early Stuarts* (Oxford, 1966) 121–32, 419.

96. 1 Will. & M. sess. 1 c. 32, sec. 12.

97. *Commons' Journals*, xi, 766, 773, cited by J. P. Cooper, 'Economic regulation and the cloth industry in seventeenth-century England', *TRHS*, 5th ser., 20 (1970) 97n.

98. 18 & 19 Chas. II c. 4; reinforced by 30 Chas. II c. 3 and 32 Chas. II c. 1.

99. 10 Will. III c. 16. See also P. Kelly, 'The Irish woollen prohibition act of 1699: Kearney re-visited', *Irish Economic and Social History*, VII (1980) 22–44.

100. 2 Will. & M. sess. 2, c. 4.

101. 11 Will. III c. 3.

102. 7 Geo. I c. 7.

103. *Cf.* E. L. Jones, 'Agricultural origins of industry', *Past and Present*, 40 (1968) 58–71.

104. A. M. Millard, Analyses of Port Books recording merchandises imported into the Port of London 1588–1640, PRO Round Room typescript 17/118, tables 11–14.

105. W. Brulez, 'Le commerce international das Pays-Bas au

XVIe siècle: essai d'appreciation quantitative', *Revue belge de philologie et d'histoire*, XLVI (1968) 1205–21.

106. E. Coornaert, *La draperie-sayetterie d'Hondschoote* (Paris, 1930) 35–43.

107. Figures printed by D. W. Jones, 'The "Hallage" Receipts of the London Cloth Markets, 1562–1720' *EcHR*, 2nd ser., XXV (1972) 569.

108. See p. 21.

109. See p. 46.

Select Bibliography

THE primary purpose of this list is to offer suggestions for further reading, but it is important to notice that it does not repeat the titles of those books and articles already listed in the notes and references section, or in the Appendix. It also indicates the authorities for most of the general statements made in the pamphlet. References to unprinted sources in the notes to the text are to documents in the Public Record Office, London, save when otherwise indicated.

The earliest account of the English woollen industry was written by John Leake *c*. 1577 and has been printed in *Tudor Economic Documents*, R. H. Tawney and E. Power (eds) (London, 1924) III, 210–25; the most recent is that by E. Lipson, *The History of the Woollen and Worsted Industries* (London, 1921). Among the many local studies might be mentioned the following: K. J. Allison, 'The Norfolk worsted industry in the sixteenth and seventeenth centuries', *Yorkshire Bulletin of Economic and Social Research*, XII (2) (1960) 73–83; H. Heaton, *The Yorkshire Woollen and Worsted Industries*, 2nd edn. (Oxford, 1965); W. G. Hoskins, *Industry, Trade and People in Exeter 1688–1800* (Manchester, 1935); N. Lowe, *The Lancashire textile industry in the sixteenth century* (Manchester, 1972); J. de L. Mann, *The cloth industry in the West of England from 1640 to 1880* (Oxford, 1971); T. C. Mendenhall, *The Shrewsbury Drapers and the Welsh wool trade in the XVI and XVII centuries* (Oxford, 1953); G. D. Ramsay, *The Wiltshire Woollen Industry in the sixteenth and seventeenth centuries*, 2nd edn (London, 1965); A. J. and R. H. Tawney, 'An occupational census of the seventeenth century', *EcHR*, V (1934–5) 25–64, which covers Gloucestershire. Many volumes of the *Victoria County Histories* contain information about local textile industries, the earliest being the contribution of G. Unwin to the Suffolk history.

There are studies of urban clothmaking centres by A. D. Dyer, *The City of Worcester in the sixteenth century* (Leicester, 1973); W. G. Rimmer, 'The evolution of Leeds to 1700', *Publications of the Thoresby Society*, L, no. 113 (1967) 91–129; W. B. Stephens, *Seventeenth-century Exeter* (Exeter, 1958); R. G. Wilson, *Gentlemen Merchants. The merchant community in Leeds 1700–1830* (Manchester,

84

1971). With regard to clothmaking or cloth-dealing firms, any list must include R. Davis, *Aleppo and Devonshire Square* (London, 1967); J. de L. Mann, 'A Wiltshire family of clothiers: George and Hester Wansey, 1683–1714', *EcHR*, 2nd ser., IX (1956–7), 241–53; ibid., *Documents illustrating the Wiltshire textile trades in the eighteenth century* (Devizes, 1964); A. Simpson, *The Wealth of the Gentry 1540–1660* (Cambridge, 1961), which includes a study of the London merchant Thomas Cullom. There are biographies of Lionel Cranfield by M. Prestwich, *Cranfield. Politics and Profits under the Early Stuarts* (Oxford, 1966), and by R. H. Tawney, *Business and Politics under James I* (Cambridge, 1958) with which might be bracketed A. F. Upton, *Sir Arthur Ingram* (Oxford, 1961), M. G. Davies has supplied an account of *The Enforcement of English Apprenticeship 1563–1642* (Cambridge, Mass., 1956), much of which concerns the textile industries. R. B. Westerfield, *Middlemen in English Business* (New Haven, Conn., 1915), includes cloth merchants in his survey. Allusions in the text to the London merchant John Isham may be checked by reference to *Two Account Books of a London merchant in the reign of Elizabeth I*, G. D. Ramsay, (ed.), Northamptonshire Record Society, XXI (1962).

Within its own field, P. J. Bowden, *The Wool Trade in Tudor and Stuart England* (London, 1962) is a reliable guide. For the new draperies, three further studies deserve mention: D. C. Coleman, 'An Innovation and its Diffusion: the "New Draperies" ', *EcHR*, 2nd ser., XXII (1969) 417–29; R. E. Pilgrim, 'The rise of the "new draperies" in Essex', *University of Birmingham Historical Journal, XII (1959–60), 36–59; N. J. Williams, 'Two documents concerning the New Draperies', EcHR*, 2nd. ser., IV (1951–2), 353–58. For knitting, there are two studies: S. D. Chapman, 'The Genesis of the British Hosiery Industry 1600–1750', *Textile History*, 3 (1972) 7–50, and J. Thirsk, 'The fantastical folly of fashion: the English stocking knitting industry, 1500–1700', *Textile History and Economic History*, N. B. Harte and K. G. Ponting (eds), (Manchester, 1973) 50–73. This volume also contains a challenging discussion of 'Textile growth' by D. C. Coleman, 1–21. There are enlivening discussions of the new draperies and of the relationship of the woollen industry to agriculture by J. Thirsk, *Economic Policy and Projects* (Oxford, 1978).

Many original documents connected with the woollen industry are printed in Tawney and Power (eds), *Tudor Economic Documents,* and in J. Thirsk and J. P. Cooper (eds), *Seventeenth-Century Economic Documents* (Oxford, 1972) and in A. E. Bland, P. A. Brown and R. H. Tawney (eds), *English Economic History, Select Documents,*

(London, 1914). Daniel Defoe, *A Tour through England and Wales,* was republished in two volumes in Everyman's Library (London, 1928) with an introduction by G. D. H. Cole.

Finally, it should be mentioned that numerous contributions bearing on the woollen industry in the early modern period are to be found in the *EcHR* (in publication since 1927) and in *Textile History* (in publication since 1968).

Index

87

Cloths, coloured   22, 63;
    German   35; homespun   32;
    medley   16, 22, 27; short   69;
    sizes   13; 'Spanish'   14, 16,
    22, 36, 37, 40; white
    undressed   47; 'wrapper',
    'double-wrapper'   74
Coal   57
Cochineal   12, 70
Cockayne Ald. Sir William   62
Colbert, French minister   37
Colchester   15, 16, 29, 40, 71
Colne valley   28
Cologne   35
Combing   10
Continental system   36
Copyholders   28
Cornwall   20
Cotton, cotton wool, cotton
    yarn   9–11, 14, 20
'Cottons'   23, 37, 66
Coventry   17, 28
Cranbrook   30
Cranfield, Lionel, earl of
    Middlesex   63, 65
Credit   55
Cromwell, Oliver   64
Cumberland, earl of   62, 63
Customs, customs duties   39, 54,
    59, 60, 64, 66, 69, 70, 73–5

Defoe, Daniel   16
Denmark   70
Derbyshire   11
Devizes   17
Devonshire   13, 14, 16, 26, 30,
    35, 37, 39
Distaff   15
Domestic system   26
Dorset   14
Drapers   11, 23, 33, 43, 52; *see
    also* London, Drapers'
    Company
Druggets   17
Dutch: competition, government,
    market   38, 64, 66, 70
Dye-house   27

Dyers, dyeing   10, 12, 22, 25,
    51, 52, 61–3
Dyestuffs   12

Earnings   27, 49
East Anglia   15, 16, 23, 30
East India Company   55, 66
Eden treaty   37
Engrossers   20
Essex   15
Exchange, bill of   54
Exeter   39

Farmer-weavers   28
Flanders   35
Flannels   36
Florence   29
France, French   10, 35, 71
Friezes   13, 23, 37
Frisadoes   15
Fuggers   69
Fullers, tuckers, fulling   24–6,
    51, 52
Fuller's earth   10
Fulling-mills   10, 26, 29
Furs   9
Fustians   20, 52

Genoa   38
Germany, Germans, German
    states   33–5, 37, 41, 49, 52; *see
    also* Hanse
Gibraltar, straits of   38
Gig-mills   11
Gloucestershire   24–8, 30
'Gloucester whites'   16
Gresham, Thomas   69
Gresham brothers   65

Hale, Sir Matthew   27
Halifax   16, 21, 23
Hallage   41, 71, 75, 77
Hamburg   37, 42, 47
Hampshire   14, 35
Hand-knitting   11, 12
Hanse, Hanseatic League   41, 54
Hereford   29

Napoleon 36
Netherlands 15, 18, 20, 33–5,
    37–9, 42, 51–3, 62, 63, 71
New Draperies 14–16, 25, 28,
    30, 34, 36, 42, 49, 61, 63, 72,
    74, 75
New World 36
Newbury 17, 25, 45, 50
Norfolk 15, 21
Norman conquest 69
North America 36
North Country 20
Northamptonshire 22, 56
Northern Europe 37
Norwich 15, 16, 29
Nottinghamshire 12
Numerals, arabic, roman 56

Old Draperies 14, 16, 25, 28,
    45, 60, 63, 66, 72, 74, 75
Oswestry 23
Ottoman empire 38
'Owling' of wool 19
Oxfordshire 30, 50

Packers 52
Pennine valley 29
Perpetuanas 16, 36, 63
Poland 35, 37
Porters 52
Portugal 35, 37, 71
Privy Council 46
Pyrenees 34

Radcliffe, City firm 45
Ragusa, Ragusans 33, 35, 38
Reading 13, 16, 29
'Readings' 14
Regraters 20
Revett, Thomas 57
Rhine, Rhineland 35, 39
Richmond and Lennox, see
    Lennox
Rouen 37
Rowing, of cloth 10
Rugs 13
Russia 37, 71

Saffron 12
Salisbury 28
Says 15, 16, 63
Scheldt, river 47, 51, 70
Scotland 37
Serges 16, 36;
Serges, Irish 66
Severn, river 28
Shalloons 17
Shears, shearers, shearing 25–7,
    49, 51, 52, 62
Shearmen 10, 11, 24, 52;
    see also London, Clothworkers'
    Company, Shearmen's
    Company
Sheep 9, 19, 20, 22, 49, 75
Shrewsbury 11, 23
Shropshire 29
Silk, silks 9, 11, 14, 53, 66, 67
Skins 9
Smithfield 32
Smuggling 67, 74; see also
    'Owling' of wool
Somerset 30
Southern Europe 35, 37
Spain, Spaniards, Spanish 12,
    13, 19, 20, 33, 35–8, 54, 70
Spanish Succession, war of
    the 36, 37
Spices 53
Spinners, spinning 21, 26, 32
Spinning-wheel 10, 15, 23, 71
Spring, Thomas 30, 45
Staplers, merchants of the Staple
    of Calais 18–21, 35, 59, 60
Steelyard 41; see also Hanse,
    Germany
Stocking-frame 11, 12
Stour valley 15
Stourbridge fair 16, 32
Stroudwater 28
'Stuffs' 16, 36, 63
Stumpe, William 25, 26
Sudbury 16
Suffolk 13, 15, 20, 30, 40
Sussex 13, 20
Switzerland 35

90